The Beginning of August

Faith for the Faithless
Hope for the Hopeless

Joe Cagliostro

IN LOVING MEMORY

Jude Phineas Cagliostro

CONTENTS

ACKNOWLEDGMENTS

The older we get, the more we realize how incapable we are of handling life's obstacles on our own. The following story would not have been possible without the loving support of my wonderful wife, Julianne. I am so blessed to have her by my side. Thank you to our children – Maggie, Wesley, Dexter, August and Daphne – for bringing so much joy into our lives. It would be impossible for me to try to name all of our friends and family that helped carry us through these difficult years. We are indebted to you for your overwhelming love and support. Many thanks to Sarah Dunlap and Todd Nicklas for taking the time to share such valuable feedback on the mess of a manuscript that I handed them. Last, but certainly not least, thanks to you, the reader.

INTRODUCTION I

Anxiety…

Despair…

Hopelessness…

Why him? Why me? Why *not* me *instead?* Why us? Why now? Why ever?

Many of us have asked these questions, desperately grasping for answers, but never expecting to find any. How does one even begin to cope with these crippling emotions while in the midst of his or her darkest days? If someone promised you an enduring hope that could carry you through those times, would you take them up on that offer? Would you even take them seriously? In an attempt to summarize what you are about to read, I will share with you a little introduction to what our family endured over the last few years. And while every family's story is unique, my prayer is that you will find similarities and through those similarities you will find comfort, encouragement and peace during some of the more difficult days in your life. I hope that no one reading this is going through dark times at this very moment, but we know that rainy days are inevitable, no matter what season we find ourselves in. To refer to hardships or any heartbreaking tragedy as a "rainy day" seems offensive, or dismissive at best, but I hope that my story will help you navigate your way through the unimaginable circumstances that you may find yourself in.

If our ability to overcome the waves of adversity and sorrow were dependent on our own strength, we would hastily drown. The message of hope that I want to offer is best described in the apostle Paul's letter to the church at Corinth when he wrote these words:

"And God said to me, 'My grace is sufficient for you, for My strength is made perfect in weakness.' Therefore, most gladly I will rather boast in my infirmities, that the power of Christ may rest upon me. Therefore, I take pleasure in infirmities, in reproaches, in needs, in persecutions, in distresses, for Christ's sake. For when I am weak, then I am strong" (2 Corinthians 12:9-10).

This personal testimony is truly an account of two absolute certainties: God's faithfulness and the power of His Word. The first half of this book will give you real, tangible examples of how we experienced the reality of a sovereign God who is more than trustworthy. The second half will remind you that the Word of God has the power to speak mightily into your life in such a way that you will never be the same again. The lessons I learned are not exclusively linked to each section. For example, God also revealed His faithfulness to us in Part II, let's call it, but He also taught us the power of His Word in Part I.

I didn't realize it early on, but I was entering into a season in my life that is best summarized by Job 1:21:

"And he said: 'Naked I came from my mother's womb and naked shall I return there. The LORD gave, and the LORD has taken away; Blessed be the name of the LORD.'"

In Part I, you will see how the Lord gave. In Part II, you will hear how He has taken away. Despite two dichotomous endings, we have learned, as Job did, to boldly and joyfully proclaim, "Blessed be the name of the Lord." I hope that you will choose to do the same.

PART I – AUGUST

This story begins as you would expect: at the end of February. We anticipated the birth of our son August to be our most memorable event of the year, but 2020 did not unfold the way we expected—for more reasons than one. If there were ever a year to tell a story about, this would be it. Not just my story, but each and every one of us could share the highs and the many lows of the dumpster fire of a year known as 2020. If you're like most people, true stories with sad endings are difficult to read and even harder to write. So many have struggled through this recent pandemic, enduring the loss of loved ones and livelihoods. Unfortunately, through these tragedies, some people whose stories were worth telling are no longer around to tell their stories. It's much easier for me to share the events surrounding the beginning of August's life because I know how amazingly it is going now. This is my feeble attempt to remind myself how God has proven Himself faithful despite my lack of faith. My prayer is that through sharing our family's frailty during this time, we would remind others that hope *can* be found in a sea of hopelessness.

So what is your story worth? Most people believe that their story is not worth telling and certainly not worth reading. I recently enjoyed a book in which the author provided a brief life story as part of its conclusion. This author's grandfather happened to be a pirate—an actual pirate! Now, *that's* a story worth reading!

I was born and raised at the Jersey Shore. I'm a nurse at a small community hospital, Monmouth Medical Center (MMC), and have been working there since 2006. My grandfather worked in real estate (the next best thing to being a pirate), and my dad ran a bicycle shop. There. That's my life story. Not very exciting, right? And I'm sure you have read some pretty incredible stories written by some pretty incredible authors. When it comes to my writing prowess, I would probably be the last person who should write a story. But who better to tell a story than the one who lived it? Who better to share the utter heartbreak and the moments of overwhelming joy than the ones who rode that rollercoaster themselves—the ones who felt the fear of that first big drop, the thrill of that fierce speed, the shock of the unexpected twists and turns, the satisfaction of knowing that they hung in there for the entire ride? But let's be honest: They (like me) may have desperately wanted to get off midway through the ride, but they were already strapped in. There was no turning back.

Through the compiling of social media posts, medical records, and reflections on Scripture and song lyrics, I want to share with you how the time surrounding the beginning of August's life consumed our lives and filled us with anxiety, fear, and hopelessness. I hope to share the growing pains that helped to define and refine our family's faith. I cannot think of a more accurate description for how God has transformed our lives through the events of the past year than 1 Peter 1:6–7: "In this you greatly rejoice, though now for a little while, if need be, you have been grieved by various trials, that the genuineness of your faith, being much more precious than gold that perishes, though it is tested by fire, may be found to praise, honor, and glory at the revelation of Jesus Christ."

A New Year

Looking back, it seems strange that life felt so normal the week before the COVID-19 pandemic hit our region. Like most years, January seemed to drag on. I recall sharing the following poem on social media on the first day of February since it felt so close to reality:

Thirty days hath September,
April, June, and November.
Unless a leap year is its fate,
February has twenty-eight.
All the rest have three days more,
Except January, which has six thousand,
One hundred and eighty-four.
–Brian Bilston

January and February marked significant moments in my extended time at MMC. This hospital played a major role in my life as it was not only where my nursing career started, but it was where my entire life began. This was where my dad, my siblings, and all of my own children were born.

In January, we had the tremendous privilege of overpacking an auditorium with hardworking healthcare workers to celebrate our hospital's designation as a Magnet facility—the highest recognition for nursing excellence. The announcement of this prestigious nursing award was met with boisterous applause. Little did we know, this would be one of the last times we packed that room for a long while.

Then, I had the bittersweet opportunity to celebrate my coworker's retirement. After working the nightshift on a medical-surgical unit for four years, I transitioned to the nursing education department in the same facility. Pat was the most influential person in my development as a nurse educator. Through our years together at MMC, she became my educator, clinical instructor, coworker, mentor, and friend. In celebration of her retirement, our department went out for a wonderful dinner at a lovely Italian restaurant. Little did I know, this would be my last time out enjoying a fun-filled evening at a restaurant for a long while.

We also celebrated my son Wesley's fourth birthday. It wasn't much of a party, but any time that our immediate family (my three siblings, my parents, and their 13 grandchildren) gets together, it's always a full house. Little did we know that this would be the last time we would have any type of gathering in our home for a long while.

My daughter, Maggie, had invited me to the Sweetheart Dance at her school for Valentine's Day. Despite never being a fan of dances when I was in high school, I was finally thrilled to attend one of these events. This event occurred during my daughter's kindergarten year. Little did we know, this school year would end like no other.

In sharing these memories, I am brought back to a time when life seemed normal. Each day was bursting at the seams with activities and people. In his third epistle, John writes the following farewell greeting, "I hope to see you shortly, and we shall speak face to face" (v. 14). If I knew that each of the aforementioned events would be the last of their kind for an indefinite amount of time, I would have valued those interactions quite differently. I would have been more careful with my words. I would have engaged in more conversations with a greater appreciation for the person I was speaking with. That's a lot of "would haves."

The Plan

A man's heart plans his way, but the Lord directs his steps.
Proverbs 16:9

The memory from early 2020 most significant to this story, however, begins with my attempt to take Maggie, my daughter, snowboarding. For months, she had been begging to go snowboarding and I finally decided that I would take off work one day to bring her. When I was a kid, my family would go on big skiing trips every year to destinations like Vermont, Maine, Colorado, or Canada. This would be Maggie's first attempt at snowboarding, so I figured a big trip like those of my childhood would have been a little premature. We decided to make our way to the American Dream, a large shopping mall with a small indoor ski slope in north Jersey.

This was the plan, but we all know what typically happens to plans. It may seem to be a recurring theme throughout this story but plans that did not go as expected actually taught us the most during these trying times. Despite the initial impulsive response of disappointment, each unexpected turn of events gave us more reason to trust in the God whom we knew had it all under control. We began to understand experientially that we did not know *what* the future holds but we know *who* holds it.

At this point, COVID-19 was all over the news, but it was not the only news. It seemed like a terrible disease that was affecting a distant land in a galaxy far, far away—too far removed to consider it a threat to the United States. A few isolated cases appeared in mid-January in the Pacific Northwest, and soon after, we heard of a few cases in the Northeast, a little closer to home. The possibility of this disease having some sort of impact on our everyday lives was becoming more of a reality.

So what happened to our snowboarding plans? Enter influenza A. Since the COVID-19 virus was not yet rampant in our region, I had no concerns that what I had was anything but the typical flu. However, the timing of this sickness could not have been worse: my wife, Juli, was going to be induced in two days. I had to get better so I could be ready for August's arrival. I typically would not have gotten tested, but in order to receive treatment to quicken my recovery, they had to confirm the diagnosis. Unfortunately, our two oldest kids also came down with the flu. And, even more devastating, when we called the hospital to inform them of my recent diagnosis, they told me that I could not come into the delivery room with my wife to be present for our son's birth.

A Little Background: Part One

For as the heavens are higher than the earth, so are My ways higher than your ways, and My thoughts than your thoughts.
Isaiah 55:9

It might be a bit of an exaggeration to say that missing the birth of my son would be devastating. I mean, I was present for the birth of our other children, so if I missed this one, three out of four really is not bad. When I first heard that I could not come to the hospital, I thought the staff couldn't be serious. Even if it was a rule, a precaution resulting from the COVID-19 pandemic, I was an employee of the hospital, and they were not about to take this moment away from me. After all, Monmouth Medical Center and I go way back.

In 1985, my mom showed up to MMC expecting to give birth to a baby. She left with two. She had no idea she was having twins. I would like to say that medical technology has come a long way since then (indeed, it has), but ultrasound technology existed back then. My mom went to all of her appointments (I think). I'm still not sure how she didn't know she was having twins. Once my brother and I were born, we went to the NICU, and I ended up with a chest tube. From what I am told, this was one of the only hospitals in the region at that time with the appropriate level of NICU care needed to provide our life-saving treatment. Our family is truly grateful for the care we received at MMC.

I also owe a great deal of gratitude to MMC for providing me with an internship between my junior and senior year of nursing school. Looking back on the journey, it's probably best that I was not allowed to be at August's birth. During my sophomore year, my first clinical rotation was in the labor and delivery department. I was scheduled to observe a C-section. I scrubbed in and gowned, gloved, and masked up. During all of my clinical hours, visual experiences never seemed to phase me, but olfactory stimuli are too much for me, especially unexpected, intense smells while I am trying to breathe through a mask (more on masks later). Perhaps you have guessed what was about to unfold. Someone should have warned me about the process of cauterization (using a heated instrument to create the incision) and the horrendous stench of burning flesh it produces. Before I knew it, I had passed out in the middle of the delivery room, and I woke up with an entire team of nurses assisting me, this poor little nursing student, out of the room.

Before moving on with my nursing career, I had to pass my NCLEX to earn my license as a registered nurse. Disappointment crushed me when I discovered that I did not pass the exam. I felt like a failure. I felt as if something was unfairly taken away from me. I began to question the career path I had chosen. The lyrics to a song hit me hard when I found myself on the losing end of this exam:

"Time I Understood?" by Wavorly

As I'm building up this house,
I wonder what of it will stay.
It seems You just take things away.
And I'll admit I shouldn't say these things.
But I have got to hear from You somehow.
Does this have a point to it?
God, I wish I could hear You.
You said You'd help me through this.
I wish You didn't have to.

Why did You take this away? I wanted it.
Show me that there is no need to be afraid.
Can I move on now that it's gone?

As I travel down this road,
I wonder if I should turn home.
All this time, I've felt alone,
My head in my hands.
Where were You when I was in need?
And I look back to find You chasing me.
Sometimes I try and I miss the point of it.
It's about time we die; we're not down here for us.

As You're tearing down this house,
There is only one thing I can say:
I'm so glad You take away,
And I'll admit things worked out for the good,
And it's about time I understood.

It's easy to blame God for not blessing us with the things in this life that we think we deserve. I slaved tirelessly through four long years of nursing school at Messiah College. I always tell people that I loved the experience, the people, the atmosphere but I would never want to do it again. I don't miss the countless hours of studying for an exam where every multiple-choice option is right and you have to decide which one is "more right," nor do I miss the early morning wake-ups for clinicals—hours that college kids didn't even know existed. In my mind, I had earned my right to pass that exam. I deserved the career path that I had prepared for and worked towards.

Written for Our Learning

For whatever things were written before were written for our learning, that we through the patience and comfort of the Scriptures might have hope.
Romans 15:4

This was just a minor setback in the grand scheme of things, but as a 22-year-old college graduate, this was one of the most devastating things that had happened to me. This was before marriage. Before kids. Before 2020. I could never have experienced the kind of loss that Job did as described in Scripture. I was convicted by Job's response when God allowed his livestock, possessions, and even his children to be taken away from him. We read that, despite his agony and seeming despair, he worshipped God (Job 1:20). The very next verse put me in the place where I knew I needed to be but wasn't sure how to get there. "And he said: 'Naked I came from my mother's womb, and naked shall I return there. The Lord gave and the Lord has taken away. Blessed be the name of the Lord" (Job 1:21). In contrast to my selfish anger, we read that "in all of this, Job did not sin nor charge God with wrong" (v. 22).

I had to begin to learn to praise God through my circumstances. The beginning of August's life was, and continues to be, a time when the Bible stories, like Job, and verses that I had learned while growing up in Sunday school started to become even more real to me. They were no longer just words that I recited so I could earn candy or a prize, but as years passed, I was reminded that the Word of God is indeed "living and powerful and sharper than any two-edged sword, piercing to the division of soul and spirit, and is a discerner of the thoughts and intents of the heart" (Hebrews 4:12). I believe the Bible is the inspired Word of God (2 Timothy 3:16), and I have personally seen the reality of this, especially in the details surrounding August's first year.

More impactful than the incredible conversations I had, text messages I received, and the songs I listened to, nothing shaped my faith more than the truths of Scripture. Nothing gave me more hope than the Word of God. Throughout these months, and heartbreak after heartbreak, I learned more of the purpose of suffering. Of course, I had read these truths many times before, but this time, I learned by *living* them. I will visit many verses that deal with sorrow and suffering in the upcoming stories, but I encourage you to look into the following passages if you are living amid a season of anguish.

- Isaiah 43:2
- John 16:33
- Romans 5:3–4
- Romans 8:18
- James 1:12

A Little Background: Part Two

Be anxious for nothing, but in everything by prayer and supplication, with thanksgiving, let your requests be made known to God; and the peace of God which surpasses all understanding, will guard your hearts and minds through Christ Jesus.
Philippians 4:6–7

By our fourth time around, we figured we had this whole pregnancy and childbirth thing down to a science. God had blessed us with three beautiful, healthy children—all with uncomplicated deliveries. Prior to the birth of our first child, however, Juli, my wife, had an ectopic pregnancy which put her at high risk for future pregnancies. This led to an abundant number of prenatal ultrasounds with our second child. By the third child, Juli no longer had these extra visits for closer monitoring of the pregnancy. During a routine check-up on our fourth, the ultrasound technician noticed larger than expected measurements on the right kidney. We were repeatedly reminded not to worry about the findings, but to have them checked out—nothing seemed alarming to us. We had been through this before and knew that we were receiving excellent care from a great team.

The first moment that anxiety started welling up inside of me occurred at the high-risk pregnancy center when the doctor gave us the name of a pediatric urologist and told us to call him immediately. We learned that we needed to make arrangements for the urologist to see August right after delivery so the doctor could evaluate him for what appeared to be hydronephrosis, or a swelling of the kidneys due to a buildup of urine.

I don't consider myself prone to anxiety, but I found the fear of the unknown overwhelming while making this phone call to arrange the in-hospital consult. In my mind, I reminded myself that this was all going to work out, reflecting on the promises found in Philippians 4:6–7, as I typically do when confronted with worries. Still, the kidney issue for our pre-born son was causing anxiety for my wife and I, and we had to bring this request for peace before God. What a challenging task to live out this verse, presenting this request "with thanksgiving." The deepest and truest peace that can only come from God through Jesus Christ was what we were longing for, but our minds and hearts were under attack with confusion, worry, and fear.

A small glimpse of that peace came when we heard that a simple outpatient surgery could resolve whatever was causing the hydronephrosis. Yet a simple outpatient surgery was only the beginning of August's long journey towards healing.

Friend

A friend loves at all times…
Proverbs 17:17

This chapter is dedicated to that friend in your life who comes to save the day. Juli has a long-lasting, intimate bond with her childhood friend Jen, who was her only non-sister in her bridal party. As Proverbs 18:24 puts it, "A man who has friends must himself be friendly, but there is a friend who sticks closer than a brother." Jen truly showed the love of a sister in such a time of need.

When I mentioned earlier that I have had to learn how to practically live out the Bible verses that I had memorized as a kid in Sunday school, I cannot emphasize enough the volumes of lessons that I have learned through the godly example of others. Friends and family had heard that I would not be allowed to witness my son's birth due to my bout with the flu. Many loved ones reached out asking how they could help and offered prayers for Juli, who was planning to deliver our son without her husband by her side. (How would she survive without me, right?) Upon hearing this, Jen called Juli, and said, "I'm on my way." Two things had to be true for this to work out: First, Jen had to be available to come. Now, Jen is a pharmacist at a large healthcare facility in central Florida, so she would have to take time off of work, schedule a flight and get here before the scheduled induction. And second, Juli had to actually want her in the room with her. If ever there were a true test of friendship, it would be if one is willing to let a friend help deliver her child.

Jen hopped on a plane and went straight to the hospital, after Juli had already arrived, to help welcome my son into the world. Words cannot express how deeply this act of love affected me. I was on the receiving end of an example of sacrificial love that most people could only dream of. Everyone needs a friend like Jen.

Even when it is not convenient, even when the travel arrangements are difficult, even if it costs you a significant amount of money, even if you have to use your vacation time, are you willing to "love at all times" (Proverbs 17:17)? That's what a friend does. She shows love, especially in the most difficult times.

When experiencing the events that I witnessed and benefiting from these great acts of love, I often begin to consider the parts of my life that have more of an eternal significance. In remembering Jen's great act of sacrificial love, I cannot help but be reminded of an even greater love as Jesus Christ spoke with His disciples in John 15:13 and declared, "Greater love has no one than this, than to lay down one's life for his friends." And yet, how often I am reminded that when Jesus Christ laid down His life on the cross so that I could receive forgiveness of sins and peace with God, He was laying down his life not just for His friends but for His enemies, too (Romans 5:10). What great love! "But God demonstrates His own love toward us, in that while we were still sinners, Christ died for us" (Romans 5:8). Am I willing and ready to show the love of Christ to those who need it most?

"Ride" by Twenty One Pilots

"I'd die for you"—that's easy to say.
We have a list of people that we would take
A bullet for them, a bullet for you,
A bullet for everybody in this room,
But I don't seem to see many bullets coming through,
See many bullets coming through.
Metaphorically, I'm the man,
But literally, I don't know what I'd do.

"I'd live for you," and that's hard to do.
Even harder to say when you know it's not true,
Even harder to write when you know it's a lie.

Who would you live for?
Who would you die for?

Little

A person's a person, no matter how small.
Theodor Seuss Geisel

Once I recovered from the flu but now tending to our two oldest kids (whom I had generously shared the infection with), I checked in with my wife to see how things were going. The doctors had begun the induction process on Thursday evening, February 27, one week before his due date, due to the concern that the baby would grow too large to deliver. As his arrival became inevitable later the next day, I had the nerve to ask my wife to hold off a few more hours so our son could be born on Leap Day. I thought that that would be pretty neat, but Juli did not find my humor the least bit entertaining. August was born around 6:00 p.m. on February 28, 2020, at a whopping 10 pounds, 2 ounces. But we couldn't call him August just yet.

We had not yet agreed on a name. When we narrowed it down to two, I preferred the name Theodore, and Juli was leaning toward August. I am glad she won since she always chooses the better names for our kids. I also liked Gideon as a first name, so Juli compromised: we made that his middle name. The naming of a new human seems strange when you think about it, but it also creates a tremendous sense of responsibility for the safety, well-being, and development of this precious life. But do the actual names even matter? As Shakespeare once said, "What's in a name? A rose by any other name would smell as sweet." As I am sure most parents have been on the receiving end of this question, people often asked us why we chose the name August Gideon. We didn't really have a good reason for the first name; we just liked it. But we settled on telling those who asked that this was the month of our wedding anniversary, and it reminds us of where this family started. (Sound convincing?) I thought the middle name—Gideon— sounded macho, but part of the reason for that choice was the story behind the name. Every other one of our kids had a family name as their middle name, but we chose a Bible name for August. So often, names in the Bible highlighted a certain quality of the individual or an aspect of his or her life.

In the Bible, the book of Judges recounts the events of specific men and women whom God raised up to intercede for His people. The nation of Israel found itself falling into a cycle of sin, captivity, repentance, and deliverance. While God's chosen people chose a life without Him, He would often allow oppressive nations to attack them and bring them into exile. When the Israelites called out to God, a mighty deliverer was needed. When God tells Gideon that he would be that one to deliver Israel from the Midianites, Gideon replies, "O my Lord, how can I save Israel? Indeed, my clan is the *weakest* in Manasseh, and I am the *least* in my father's house?" (Judges 6:15) His response might sound all too familiar to those of us who have wanted to shirk responsibility. This judge claims his life is too insignificant to amount to anything. How can such an irrelevant man accomplish anything relevant? Yet, despite his self-pitying mindset and overwhelming sense of insignificance, God reaffirms that He will use him to deliver the Israelites.

With very little insight into the trials that our little August would have to face, we were reminded of the promises of God—that He could use someone as "little" as Gideon to accomplish great things. Our little warrior reminded us that no obstacle is too large for our God to overcome. At the hospital where I work, I would often see a small decoration in the gift shop as I walked by each day. It reminded me, "Don't tell God about your big problems. Tell your problems about your big God." August had to overcome bigger problems from a physical perspective than my wife or I had ever dealt with. For anyone who has had a child go through sickness or surgeries, it is heart-wrenching to watch them go through it, and as their parents, we would do anything to take their place. We hope and pray that the troubles August has overcome in his time on earth so far are a foreshadow of his victories in bigger, eternal matters as he grows into a mature, young man.

The Birth

When a woman is giving birth, she has sorrow because her hour has come,
but when she has delivered the baby, she no longer remembers the anguish,
for joy that a human being has been born into the world.
John 16:21

I don't know much about what happened the day our son entered this world, but I think it went fairly well. Jen was a champ and did a much better impression of a doula than I could have done. It felt strange to meet my son via a video call and not actually see him until two days after he was born. I was able to pick up my wife and son the Sunday afternoon following his birth. A quick snuggle with him in the hospital room before making a luggage trip to the parking garage was enough to hold me over until we arrived home. Jen would spend the night before flying back to Florida the next day, and the rest of our kids were incredibly excited to meet their baby brother. Despite the busyness and commotion of our first night together as a new and improved family of six, I—still in recovery mode from the flu—nearly passed out on the couch. Before falling asleep, I held my son once more. This would be the last time I would do so for the next few months. Soon, I would wish I had cherished it more.

As I wrote that sentence, I thought back to a recent funeral I had attended. Close friends had been shocked by the sudden passing of one of their two-month-old twins while he slept. When I reflect on the difficulty of being unable to hold my son for a few months, my prayers go out to this family who will never again hold theirs. Despite this tragedy falling upon their family, they have shown that not even the greatest moments of devastation can shake the rock-solid foundation of a family whose faith and hope is built on the Lord Jesus Christ and the promises found in the Word of God. They reminded me of the importance of appreciating hugs, of taking pictures, of making sure that Mom and Dad and siblings cherish every moment that they are given with their loved ones. And they shared with me the historical account of Job (whom I referenced earlier), a man who lost everything including his children. His response can serve as a reminder and challenge to all of us when we feel as if something has been wrongfully taken from us. "The Lord gave and the Lord has taken away; Blessed be the name of the Lord" (Job 1:21). After attending the funeral, my three-year-old asked why the family was happy. I asked him what he meant, and he shared that he saw the family smiling. My friend had the opportunity to do something I could never imagine doing: sharing the eulogy at his son's funeral. Despite expressing their deep sorrow and overwhelming heartbreak, they shared the hope and assurance that they have fully placed their trust in: a salvation that rests on the finished work of a loving Savior. A Savior who sacrificed His life and rose again victoriously so that all who believe could have hope in His name.

Looking back in light of this recent event, the momentary separation from August seems like a hardship that was nothing my God was unable to carry me through. Is it not true that when we are facing a struggle, it feels like nothing could be more debilitating or devastating? Holding your newborn child in your arms is something pretty special. Whether it is your first child or your fifth, your first time holding him or her or your 500th time hugging them, cherish it. "Now may the God of hope fill you with all joy and peace in believing, that you may abound in hope by the power of the Holy Spirit" (Romans 15:13).

Urology

As soon as we found out about August's condition from the prenatal ultrasound, we arranged for a visit from a local, well-respected pediatric urology group upon our son's arrival. Every person and professional contact we had recommended this group without reservations. They came to see August the day after he was born, and the ultrasound confirmed what they had suspected: The obstruction of urine flow was caused by swelling at the end of a ureter where it entered the bladder, known as a right-sided ureterocele. They also identified a "duplex kidney," or the presence of an additional ureter, commonly associated with ureteroceles. The urology team recommended surgery as soon as possible, so we scheduled an appointment for the following week in preparation.

A few days later, my in-laws arrived, and my mother-in-law accompanied my wife and I to the urology appointment. We had no idea how rare having multiple family members present at an office visit would be in the days to come. During the visit, the urologist explained that the surgical intervention was a common and fairly straightforward outpatient procedure. This is where things began to get interesting.

The doctor was repeatedly interrupted and had to step out of the office a number of times during the visit. COVID-19 cases had begun to overwhelm the healthcare systems in New York and northern Jersey. As the cases began to invade our region of central New Jersey, some major changes were taking place. All elective surgeries at Monmouth Medical Center were being cancelled as staff and rooms were being reallocated to care for COVID-19 patients. The pediatric unit was in the process of being converted into an adult ICU unit to care for the influx of COVID-19 patients. This should not have impacted our situation since the surgery was scheduled as an outpatient case, but for the surgery to move forward, the urologist required an available inpatient pediatric unit to admit August to in the event of potential complications or the need for closer observation. The urologist was getting repeated calls regarding the cancellation of all elective surgeries. The need to correct August's kidney and bladder issue was considered *urgent* and fell somewhere in between *elective* and *emergent*. A major delay in correcting the issue could result in recurrent kidney infections, and if the urine was refluxing up the ureters to the kidneys, there was potential for permanent kidney damage as well. Now that my employer no longer had an available unit and was only performing emergent cases, the surgery had to be rescheduled at another local hospital. This is when we entered into one of the more frightening areas of health care: insurance.

Insurance

Fear not, for I am with you; Be not dismayed, for I am your God; I will strengthen you,
I will help you, I will uphold you with My righteous right hand.
Isaiah 41:10

Another reason that we chose the pediatric urologist that we did, besides their outstanding reputation, was the fact that they were covered by our insurance. When it comes to matters of health insurance, I seldom venture into that realm by choice. In fact, I believe most of us do our best to avoid having to deal with our health insurance. While I am indeed grateful for the coverage we have, it comes with its share of headaches. Now that our son's surgery was rescheduled for another local hospital, we had concerns about this facility, despite it's good reputation, since it was part of a competing healthcare system.

There is an interesting thing about working in health care and having my insurance provided by the hospital that I work for. The coverage, the value, and the benefits are excellent—as long as you stay in the network. Once you step out of that network, it's as if you have committed the most heinous crime. If we were to have the repair of August's ureterocele performed at Monmouth Medical Center, the surgery and hospital stay would have been covered by insurance, with the possibility of not even owing a copay. Due to the closure of the inpatient pediatric unit, the surgery that was now scheduled at this out-of-network facility was going to cost us at least $10,000 out of pocket. It blew my mind that the same doctors performing the same surgery at a location just 20 minutes down the road would make a drastic difference. I immediately got on the phone with my insurance.

Let me pause to share again that I am extremely grateful for the insurance coverage we do have. I remind myself that many people out there do not have good insurance plans or any health coverage at all, for that matter. Also, you cannot put a price tag on your child's health. We would be willing to pay any price for our son to be healthy. But, if we had the choice between having the same procedure done for free versus paying that ridiculous price, after long and careful consideration, I am pretty sure we would choose the free route. How much would you be willing to pay for the healing of your child? Have you ever thought about putting a price on it? I'm reminded of the words of Psalm 49:7–8, which tells us, "Truly, no man can ransom another, or give to God the price of his life; for the redemption of their souls is costly." Many people say that they would give their very own lives for their child or loved one, but the reality is we could never pay the price for the eternal, spiritual redemption of another. But we can be grateful that Christ was able and willing to give His life for us. We were indeed bought with a tremendous price, and we have not been redeemed with corruptible things "but with the precious blood of Christ, like that of a lamb without blemish or spot" (1 Corinthians 6:20; 1 Peter 1:18–19).

While some may hesitate to pay a hefty price even for something or someone we love, God "spared not His Son" to deliver us from our sin (Romans 8:32).

All of these thoughts aided me in gaining the proper perspective on this whole situation. I had to realize that either I would be inquiring, and in all sincerity, fighting, to not have to pay the large sum for this surgery or say that no price would keep me from doing what was in the best interest of August. However, I still did what I despise doing: I called my health insurance.

I explained that we had selected our specific pediatric urologist based on the fact that we had every intention of having the surgery done where I worked. This group had privileges there, and they were covered by our insurance. I told the representative that due to the COVID-19 pandemic, the healthcare systems in the northern part of New Jersey were already overwhelmed. This caused the closure of our pediatric unit (pediatric patients were being diverted to a facility within the system that could accommodate a larger pediatric patient population) and the cancellation of all elective cases at my smaller community hospital. August needed surgery and our only option now was to have it done at the neighboring hospital with a pediatric unit. Once again, the expectation for this surgery was that it was to be an outpatient procedure, but the surgeons required an available inpatient pediatric unit in the event that August would need to stay overnight. I asked the insurance representative if they had some sort of "pandemic clause" that allowed me to submit a claim for the surgery to be covered. The representative responded apologetically that nothing could be done and we would have to pay the full price of the surgery out of pocket.

I did my best to maintain my composure, but I felt a wide range of emotions sweeping through me. Was I angry? Yes. Confused? Yes. Sad? Frustrated? Concerned? Overwhelmed? Desperate? Looking back, I think one of the best words to describe how I was feeling is *dismayed*. By definition, to be dismayed is to cause one to lose courage or resolution. I had lost what little courage I had. We were far from a resolution. I was perturbed. Unsettled. Anxious, even. In my selfish arrogance, I pride myself on being the non-anxious person in my family. By God's grace, my wife and I balance each other out, and since she often worries enough for the two of us, I overcompensate (to a fault) by being indifferent oftentimes (especially when I shouldn't be). For the first time in a really long time, I felt as if things were completely out of my control, and I was indeed dismayed. I was desperately in need of the reminder in Isaiah 41:10, "Fear not, for I am with you; Be not dismayed, for I am your God; I will strengthen you, I will help you, I will uphold you with My righteous right hand." But I was not ready to believe it.

Antibiotic

When Jesus heard that, he said to them, "Those who are well have no need of a physician, but those who are sick."
Matthew 9:12

We continued to go to the same pediatric urologist and explained our current situation. Due to the nature of August's disorder and the uncertainty of when the other hospital would cancel all their elective surgeries, we scheduled to have his surgery in the next two weeks, hoping and praying that we would find a way for our insurance to at least partially pay for the procedure. In the meantime, August had started an antibiotic the day he was born to prevent any type of urinary tract infections. We were told that a prophylactic antibiotic is routinely given as a preventative measure due to the high likelihood of recurrent UTIs. In one of our follow-up visits during those very busy first few weeks of Augie's life, the urologist told us that she wanted to continue the antibiotic. She wrote the prescription, and I headed over to Walgreens. I got in the massively long line—many people were beginning to socially distance due to the first reports of multiple COVID-19 cases in our region. When I approached the pharmacist and handed him the prescription, he asked me which dose I wanted. I was surprised by this question, and I informed him that we were told to continue his preventative dose of the antibiotic. The pharmacist informed me that the prescription was for a *treatment* dose, which was much larger than the prophylactic one. I asked him to refill the old prescription; I explained the urologist wanted him to "continue what he was on." Now is the moment when you can call me a terrible nurse. What type of healthcare professional blindly gets a prescription filled without looking at the details? The urologist had written a prescription for the wrong dose, and if it hadn't been for the pharmacist questioning the change in dose, we would have given our son the treatment dose for a UTI he didn't have. We were already concerned because we had been told to anticipate our son taking antibiotics daily for the first two years of his life. Now, the doctor had mistakenly prescribed the wrong dose!

As soon as I got home, I called the office to express my concerns. Keep in mind that we were already overwhelmed with the impending surgery for our son. My conversation with the doctor went quite well. He was very apologetic, assuring me that he would follow up with the provider who prescribed the wrong dose. At this point, our confidence in this group was beginning to waver significantly. With not-so-high hopes, I began to think that looking into other pediatric urologists might be worthwhile. My initial thought was how challenging it would be to find a new doctor who could get August in for surgery sooner rather than later, but we figured it would not hurt to look. And, when you are a nurse educator working in a hospital, you do the only thing you know how to do: ask your nurse friends for advice.

The Merger

Let us hold fast the confession of our hope without wavering,
for He who promised is faithful.
Hebrews 10:23

Despite my lack of faith in finding another pediatric urologist, I started with two of my coworkers who were pediatric nurse educators. They immediately recommended the group that we were currently seeing. After explaining our situation with the insurance and COVID-19 forcing our son's surgery out of network, my coworker Gail reached out to a few of her pediatric nurse educator counterparts within our system.

As I shared earlier, we wanted to stay in-network in order to limit the cost of the surgery (and possibly have insurance cover it completely). In 2016, the Barnabas Health System merged with the Robert Wood Johnson Health System to create the RWJBarnabas network, the most comprehensive health system in New Jersey at that time. Due to the merger, Gail could contact a few pediatric nurse educators at the RWJ New Brunswick Campus. They provided the name of Dr. Joseph Barone. This pediatric urologist was not as well-known in our local area since he practiced at the hospital about an hour north of us. We reached out to the office to see if our son could be seen by this doctor and be scheduled for surgery as soon as possible. We were amazed to find out that we could get an appointment on the same day that August was tentatively scheduled for his surgery at the out-of-network facility. This was an answer to prayer and a glimmer of hope in getting August the corrective procedure that he needed to preserve his kidney. It's funny how this merger had been a point of frustration for me as an employee. Now that I realized how it more than doubled the number of in-network providers and made a very reputable urologist available to us, my perspective changed dramatically. At times, we can't see the forest for the trees and so was the case for us here. In the end, I can safely say, yes, I am indeed grateful for the merger.

The Wave

My God shall supply all my need according to His riches in glory.
Philippians 4:19

With a newborn at home and a novel coronavirus taking over our area (and our hospital), we had concerns about the possibility of being infected with and transmitting this virus, which healthcare experts knew very little about. We had seen the devastation that it caused in other parts of the world and the way that experts were frantically searching for and debating what treatments would be the most effective. The last thing we wanted was to bring any sort of infection into our home. We thought that the best approach, for the moment at least, was to separate as much as possible. This would not have been even a remote possibility if it were not for my in-laws having arrived a few days before the "world shut down." Interstate travel was being banned, and my father-in-law, who worked for a South Florida school system, found out that work was put on hold since the schools had shut down for the foreseeable future.

While an inconvenience to my in-laws (who, I am sure, were thrilled to spend some extra time with their new grandson), their visit was a blessing to our family. At the same time, my hospital was offering their employees free rooms at a local hotel to reduce the spread of COVID-19 among their families. Each of these circumstances allowed my family and me to temporarily separate, given the many questions about this virus. Many of my coworkers also took advantage of these accommodations to protect their families from the unknown.

Now, don't get me wrong. It was definitely a challenge to not see my family, especially my son who I had only been around for about a week, but the Wave hotel that the hospital offered was a slight improvement to the sunken-in couch in our freezing unfinished basement. I ended up splitting my time between the hotel and the basement primarily due to meals and laundry needs. I felt as if I were living two different lives simultaneously. One day, I would be riding a bike along the boardwalk or walking on the sand at a beachfront hotel with a king-size bed all to myself. The very next night, I was sleeping on a couch in my basement with a space-heater six inches from my feet with food being tossed down the dungeon stairs so I didn't starve. To clarify, the food was never actually "tossed" down, and it was the finest dungeon food that one could ever imagine. I may have lived like a king at the Wave hotel, but I ate like a king in my basement thanks to the wonderful cooking of my mother-in-law.

Through the provision of the hotel and the presence of my in-laws, God was indeed providing for all of our needs, and we were especially grateful to have the additional help available to us. He was working out everything more perfectly than we could have planned (Romans 8:28). My drive home from work each day brought me to two alternating locations, but the one constant was a longing for my family. The first few days were peaceful and full of rest, but that got old quick. I wanted to be with my family. I wanted to hold my new son. I wanted to hug my wife. All in time.

The In-Laws

So Moses listened to the voice of his father-in-law and did all that he said.
Exodus 18:24

In-laws are the best. While households were isolating from each other, we were thrilled to have them with us. In addition to my wife getting to spend some extended quality time with her parents, their love and support was beyond measure, and we can never repay them for the help that they provided. Beyond the meals and laundry and diapers and bedtime stories, Malcolm and Joann were excellent company for Juli and the kids. It felt strange that during such a crazy and confusing time as this, our kids were having the time of their lives! Their questions about the virus would come later: How long is this going to last? When can I go back to school? Why can't we go anywhere? Our four-year-old was the maker of future plans as every other sentence out of his mouth started with "When the coronavirus is over."

But in the first two months, they were loving it. They probably had more fun with Papa and Mimi (Malcolm and Joann) than with Daddy, so I probably should have been upset or offended or convicted that I wasn't doing a good enough job as their father. But I appreciated the love that was bursting out of that house. I still tried to be extra cautious whenever I would come to the house, spending time outside in the driveway or the backyard before making my way to the basement. We shared an Easter meal while I joined remotely from the basement. Despite the unusual circumstances, it was a great memory. I also missed the opportunity to teach Wesley how to ride a bike, but my father-in-law took care of it for me. These are memories that I know will stick with the kids, and I know they will remember how much love was poured out on them from my mother- and father-in-law.

We had some great conversations too. COVID-19 was obviously a topic that consumed a decent amount of conversation time, but our talks went well beyond that. Malcolm has a genuine love and interest in people. I am a nurse with a lot less life experience than him (perhaps a lot less love and interest in people, too, but there is always room to grow). We shared our perspectives on the pandemic and the various ways that people were choosing to go about their lives. I shared some of my experiences from the hospital, and he provided insight from a non-healthcare perspective. When you are working in the hospital on these COVID-19 units, you see the worst of the worst, and that can definitely change your perspective—for better or worse. It was great to get fresh insight from my father-in-law, and I believe through our many conversations we both gained a new perspective and appreciation that we had not had before. Despite having opinions on opposite ends of the spectrum at times, we talked through some of the challenging societal changes that were progressing on a daily basis and learned from one another.

Due to my parents' health conditions and the fact that they had their own home down the street, my family was keeping their distance from them for the time being and sticking around the house as much as possible. I remember multiple conversations with coworkers at the hospital when I first started working there. Many of them were the first generation in their family to come to the United States from the Philippines, India, Ghana, China, or other parts of the world. The message was the same from all of them: "Make sure you appreciate having family nearby." This was something that I took for granted, until I was able to experientially understand what my coworkers were talking about. It truly is a blessing to have them close by. May we learn to appreciate family more and more and show our appreciation in practical ways.

Cross-Training

Everyone should eat and drink, and find enjoyment in all his labor,
for these things are a gift from God.
Ecclesiastes 3:13

Reflecting on my time as a nightshift telemetry nurse, almost every shift was filled with "emergencies." The definition of *emergency* can vary greatly from one patient to another. Whether a patient was suffering from a life-threatening, uncontrolled irregular heart rhythm or requesting fresh ice water and an extra pillow, an emergency is whatever the patient defines it to be. Sort of like how a patient's reported pain had been defined in recent years as "whatever the patient says it is." When I left bedside nursing and moved into my educational role, I assumed that I would no longer have to deal with such emergencies. Long gone were the days of breaking a sweat at work, or so I thought.

While working in nursing education, naturally, there was an emphasis on continuing nursing education and professional development. On several occasions, I attended conferences that warned nurse educators to always be prepared for educational emergencies. Many of us scoffed at the idea and thought that this was not a possibility. How in the world could the provision of education be considered a true emergency? Enter the COVID-19 pandemic. In a similar fashion to how August's "urgent" surgery was not considered "emergent" and, thus, was delayed until further notice, all non-emergent surgeries at MMC were canceled. This left hundreds of nurses and techs who typically worked in the operating room, the post-anesthesia care unit, outpatient surgery, and other procedural areas with no work. In the non-surgical departments of the hospital, the nurses and techs were feeling the pressure of being understaffed while caring for patients suffering and dying from a disease that the medical experts knew very little about.

With less than a two-week notice of an impending surge of COVID-19 patients, we had to prepare our facility and our staff to care for critically ill patients infected with a contagious virus that had already wreaked havoc on other parts of the world. To say that the turnaround for making changes in a hospital is not always the quickest would be an understatement. For example, I was hired in 2007, and my unit had a broken drawer at its nurses' station. More than 14 years later, that drawer is still broken. However, in those two weeks, we added windows to patients' rooms, installed outlets, added negative pressure capabilities to every room in the intensive care unit, and converted our pediatric unit into an adult ICU.

Beyond pulling former ICU nurses from case management and other nonclinical areas back to the bedside and reviewing checklists of skills that some of these nurses had not used in more than 20 years, we also had to cross-train nurses who had no critical-care experience to work in our ICU and emergency department. Nurses from perioperative services, outpatient-care areas, women's services, and pediatrics had to attend a crash course on caring for COVID-19 patients. One major problem: we still had to put the course together. Thus, I experienced my first educational emergency.

With all of our critical-care resources being pulled, I had to take the material that was provided to me from our infection prevention department and critical-care educators to come up with a one-day course on caring for the COVID-19 patient. With classroom limitations created due to enforced social distancing, these classes were offered for approximately three weeks. A few challenges were presented during this time. The guidelines and recommendations were constantly changing, as often as three times in one day. When I taught the proper donning and doffing of personal protective equipment (PPE) and which PPE to use at the beginning of the day, I would often have to clarify what was taught due to new regulations by the end of the class. Isolation precautions were constantly shifting. Available supplies were always changing. Our respiratory therapists provided resources for training on the use of high-flow oxygen as well as ventilator and airway management.

I was used to teaching full-day classes a few times each week, but the strain on your voice due to talking nonstop for five days straight is challenging, as any teacher can tell you. I was not used to this. In addition to that, the mask mandate was a new factor to consider. I had to learn to speak loud enough that my muffled voice could be heard through my mask, and I will admit I slowly mastered the non-fogging-glasses-while-masking technique. Through all of these difficulties, I had to remind myself of Ecclesiastes 3:13, which reminds us to "find enjoyment in all [our] labor" because it is a "gift from God." For many of us, work can seem like a drag, and we often don't feel like going back after a miserable day. Despite the frustrations and the unanswered questions, I knew that many people were out of work as "nonessential" businesses were shut down. The fact that I still had a steady source of income to provide for my family and their needs when so many others were in a desperate and uncertain position truly put things into perspective for me in recognizing every provision as a blessing from God.

In the Sunshine and the Sorrow

In everything give thanks, for this is the will of God in Christ Jesus for you.
1 Thessalonians 5:18

Circumstances do not always lead someone's heart to a place of sincere gratitude. In fact, they will often drag us to a state of discontentment complete with grumbling and complaining. Such was the tendency of my own heart in dealing with this pandemic. I was not forced to separate from my family, but we believed it to be the wisest decision since so much was still unknown about this novel coronavirus. It was difficult to be away from Juli and the kids, especially August—I had not even spent a week with him, and now, we were going on two months where I could not hold my son. However, I was constantly reminded of 1 Thessalonians 5:18, "In everything give thanks; for this is the will of God in Christ Jesus for you." Was it God's will to have me separated from my family? Was it His will for the amount of death we were seeing in our hospital, more than I had seen in all of my years working there? Was it His will for this virus to take away lives and tear apart families? I may never understand many things, but in considering the events of 2020 and beyond, I saw God's hand working behind the scenes and in broad daylight. Sometimes, I really had to stop and consider how to find God's divine intervention in everything while, at other times, His providence smacked me in the face. So often, He reminded me that He was in control. He had it all worked out. I didn't have to worry about the details. He had it covered.

But why should we give thanks? No one can force you to have a thankful heart; it is something that each person must decide. If giving thanks in all circumstances is His will, shouldn't that cause me to endure whatever hardships may come, even if there is no end in sight? Hebrews 10:35–36 commands us to "not cast away your confidence, which has great reward. For you have need of endurance, so that after you have done the will of God, you may receive the promise." The fulfillment of that promise has much to do with the culmination of our faith in the Lord Jesus Christ. Despite how hopeless life may seem at times, we have an eternal reward if we live by faith in the One who is coming again for us.

So many clouds, but so many silver linings. I was separated from my wife and newborn, but my in-laws were somehow "stuck" in New Jersey for a few months. Juli had the support that she needed, and I was able to focus on the increased demands of work. I was trying to avoid bringing any sickness home, and my hospital provided a placed to stay: A luxury beachfront hotel.

The Wave Resort was a recently constructed resort that offered spacious rooms and balconies with beautiful views of the ocean. The only downfall was that while the majority of my coworkers ended up with an ocean view, I ended up on the other side of the building with a balcony view of a construction site. In everything give thanks, I reminded myself.

Growing up five minutes from the beach, I never had much of an appreciation for it. I remember many trips to the ocean when I was a little boy, but as I grew older, it lost its appeal. Stuck at a hotel on the beach left me plenty of time to regain that appreciation for the beauty and peacefulness of the region I called home. With more time alone than I had had since before Juli and I had kids, I had more time to think. More time to run. More time for bike rides on the boardwalk. More time for slow walks on the beach. I found myself strolling the beach many afternoons after work, listening to the waves crash on the shore. God reminded me that He was in control of this whole mess and that I would need endurance. One afternoon, I was listening to an album by Rend Collective, which reminded me of whom I could trust and how to respond in times like these.

"Life Is Beautiful" by Rend Collective

How can it be, You know my name?
Tamer of storms who calms the waves,
How can it be, I can't explain,
Why You carry me and all my shame.
You take my sin and all of the mess
As far as the east is from the west.
Everything changed, I stand amazed.
My every breath is grace.
I will not waste this day You've made;
I will be glad
Rejoice, rejoice, in the sunshine, in the sorrow,
Oh, my soul rejoice.
Rejoice, rejoice, in the trial, in the trouble,
Oh, my soul rejoice.

An Attitude of Gratitude

*Giving thanks always for all things to God the Father
in the name of our Lord Jesus Christ.*
Ephesians 5:20

The second-best thing besides the beach at the Jersey Shore (or the best thing, depending on your perspective) is the food. I spent a few years of my life in the southern side of central Pennsylvania, and while it is indeed a beautiful place that offers a much-needed change of pace, nothing can compare to the food at the Jersey Shore. During this time of the COVID-19 pandemic, the generosity and kindness of some of the local businesses was on full display at Monmouth Medical Center. Local barbecue, Mexican, pizza, sub, and cake joints donated an incredible amount of food. Every staff member in the hospital was able to eat to their hearts content and not some lousy south-central Pennsylvania pizza but really good Jersey Shore nourishment. Not to mention, the best Italian ice you could ever dream of was delivered right to my office! I felt like Moses when he had to tell the Israelites to stop bringing their contributions because the people were bringing more than enough for the construction of the tabernacle (Exodus 36:5). We literally had to tell restaurants to stop sending food because we did not want to waste it. Appreciation (and lack thereof) for healthcare workers became a hot topic as the pandemic ran through the country. Perhaps I won't even get to that part of the story, but at this point, we felt the love of the community around us. When Nurses' Week came, we felt it even more.

At the very onset of the pandemic to our region, like many other regions, "nonessential" businesses were shut down. As I mentioned earlier, I had to learn to view the impact of the pandemic from the perspective of a small business owner. My older brother had his bike shop business, which my dad had opened in 1975, and many others like him personally saw the effects of the pandemic. From a personal perspective, every local business owner would consider his or her business essential—essential in providing for their families, essential for making ends meet.

These small bursts of sunshine through the clouds in the form of local businesses' generosity really called on me to be grateful, but I also realized that in Scripture, we are not just told to give thanks *in* everything but *for* everything (1 Thessalonians 5:18; Ephesians 5:20). I should not just maintain the mindset of "Life might be pretty miserable right now, but I am sure that I can find something to be thankful for in this situation." Rather, I should cultivate a mindset of giving thanks *for* all things. When I spend twice as many hours at work, I need to be thankful *for* that. When I am drenched in sweat under multiple layers of full body PPE to enter a COVID-19 patient's room, I need to be thankful *for* that.

How can someone who is suffering from COVID-19 be thankful *for* COVID-19? How can someone who lost a loved one due to COVID-19 be thankful *for* that? I can't answer all of these questions, but my mind goes back to an article that I read in a missionary magazine. A family was displaced from their own country due to oppression and threats of violence at the hands of ISIS. A number of their relatives had already been killed by this terrorist group, and those remaining were fleeing for their lives. Through the hunger, thirst, pain, and suffering, the family arrived at a refugee camp on the country's border. In this camp, they had their physical needs met, and the missionaries who provided the material blessings also offered something far greater than anything this world can offer. They shared the hope that they have in the risen Savior who had suffered and died on the cross for their sins. This family whose lives were filled with all sorts of turmoil finally found peace and hope in the name of the Lord Jesus Christ. The mother of this family replied, "I thank God *for* ISIS. If it were not for ISIS, we would not have fled to this refugee camp, and we would never have come to know the peace and hope that is found through faith in Christ."

What a perspective! I know that COVID-19 has had a devastating effect on so many people's lives, and I am not here to dictate that anyone *must* find a way to give thanks for all of the suffering. But I know that there is hope that stretches beyond this life in the One who is sovereign over all of the confusion and sadness and despair. *In* Him and *for* Him, I give thanks.

A Reason to Hope

But sanctify the Lord God in your hearts, and always be ready to give a defense to everyone who asks you a reason for the hope that is in you, with meekness and fear.
1 Peter 3:15

Every day at work presented new challenges. Our department's ability to support the bedside staff became increasingly more difficult as we struggled to keep up with the ever-changing recommendations. The type of isolation was changing on a daily basis. The type of PPE required and available was different every day it seemed. The very first weekend that COVID-19 patients started to arrive at our hospital, staff were told to not wear masks since there was a growing concern from the northern part of the state regarding a shortage of supplies. By Monday, everyone had been told to wear a standard surgical mask, but not an N95. Once again, the conservation of resources was cited as the reason. By Tuesday, everyone was wearing N95s. This fluctuation in standards would continue over the next few months, whether related to new research or availability of supplies.

Ensuring the availability of supplies on each COVID-19 unit became a challenge. Some of my time was spent replenishing supplies when a particular area was running out. During one of my trips to gather more supplies, I was able to have a conversation with one of the staff members who works in materials management. We asked each other how we were holding up and how our families were doing. He shared that his family was well, but like most of us, he had this overwhelming anxiety regarding the severity of the pandemic, the right methods of keeping him and his family safe, and how to talk about it with his kids. I shared that I had some of the same questions and that there were many questions we didn't have the answers to. However, I also shared where my hope was truly resting. We can try to do everything right in facing this virus head-on and trying to protect ourselves and our families and yet still succumb to it. I told him that I had come to learn that putting our faith in anything in this life would always leave us disappointed. This life is temporal. If we put our hope in things that are passing, our hope will expire along with what we put our hope in. I spoke of the hope I have in Christ. "We can say with confidence, 'The Lord is my helper; I will not fear. What can man do to me?'" (Hebrews 13:6) What can this virus do to me? Sure, it can ravage this life and even take it away, but it cannot touch the confidence that I have in Christ and the peace and hope that He brings in this life and the life to come. This coworker of mine asked how I was processing and handling the whole situation and I was able to give him the reason for the hope that was in me (1 Peter 3:15).

Perfect Timing

At this point, you may be asking yourself, "Isn't this story about August? When does the cute little guy come back into the picture?" Up to this point, August was seemingly out of the picture for me. I was thankful to have a full team of family members caring for him while my work responsibilities sucked every ounce of energy from me. In the following chapters, I have recorded a number of other life events interspersed throughout all of August's complex care that had a pretty significant impact on our lives. Rest assured, my son was constantly on my mind. The time came for my in-laws to leave, and I will tell you that this was met with mixed emotions. Juli and I knew that it was probably not the wisest choice for me to continue to isolate from my family for an extended period if she was home with our newborn and three other children. We prayed about it and decided that once my in-laws left, I would go home. We would trust the Lord to give us the protection we needed while I continued to spend time at the hospital, oftentimes on COVID-19 units.

In regard to timing, the occurrence of a pandemic is never convenient. However, if you ever plan on having a baby, at the beginning of a pandemic may not be entirely a bad thing. In considering the potential seriousness of August's issues, we realized that any sort of sickness could send him to the hospital. The pandemic along with its "shelter in place" and quarantine demands helped limit August's exposure to potential sickness. Otherwise, the timing of everything was far from convenient and put a real wrench in our plans.

So we developed a plan. Despite its high taxes and other unsavory characteristics (feel free to mentally develop a long list), New Jersey has a few things going for it (I already mentioned the food). In 2019, the NJ government had decided to extend its family leave policy from six weeks to 12 weeks. This meant that following the birth of a child, fathers could take up to 12 weeks of paid "paternity" leave to bond with and care for their child. Paternity leave can be taken at any point before the baby's first birthday. I won't say that this change had any impact on our decision to have another child (it really did not), but I would be lying if I said it did not cross my mind as one of the perks. The law was not going to take effect until July 1, 2020. Enter our plan:

1. Have baby
2. Work until July 1.
3. Go to reunion in Ohio and show off August to relatives.
4. Drive to Florida.
5. Spend a month visiting family and soaking up the sun.
6. Drive home.
7. Address home renovation projects for the next six weeks.
8. Go back to work.

Sounds wonderful, right? Well, due to my in-laws' departure and August's need to have his scheduled surgery by May, I knew I would need to start my family leave before July 1. This meant I would get the six-week leave instead of the 12-week leave. I was sure to ask the state if I could get the additional six weeks of leave after July 1, but they told me that would not be possible. I am indeed grateful for the time I could take off because, when the time came, it allowed me to be available to stay with August for each of his surgeries. I did not know that he would end up spending approximately a quarter of his first year of life in the hospital, but God knew, and He worked it out better than we could have imagined.

I came home in May, after more than two months of separation, to reclaim my house (and my family) on the day that my in-laws were leaving. Any concern we had for COVID-19 was temporarily erased from our minds as we enjoyed a sweet reunion. Despite frequent trips to the driveway and keeping my distance in the backyard, I felt as if I had not seen my family in a lifetime. Maybe it's just the Italian in me speaking, but you never realize how much you miss a warm hug from a loved one until you're separated. Those were the best hugs that I ever received.

I knew my family had been well cared for. They ate like royalty. The laundry never backed up. Wesley learned how to ride a pedal bike. He was thrilled to show me how fast he could go around our driveway. In our family of bicycle enthusiasts, if you're not riding a bike by the age of four, you're in serious trouble. You are practically disowned. And using training wheels as a part of the process is an unspeakable violation. How embarrassing for me, as a father, that I have never been able to teach my kids how to ride a bike. Maggie learned from Aunt Kristin. Wesley learned from Papa. And soon, Dexter would learn, but not from his dad. Of course not. Maggie would teach him. Anyway, it just felt good to be together as a family. We knew there were a lot of uncertainties, but we also knew we would be fine—even if we didn't have all of the answers.

I'm Loving It

The man of God answered, "The LORD is able to give you much more than this."
2 Chronicles 25:9b

The concern of not having August's surgery covered by insurance had passed, and we were quite relieved to have avoided that financial burden. The in-network pediatric urologist that a coworker recommended was able to schedule an appointment and, ultimately, a tentative surgery date, pending the current COVID-19 situation. We knew that outside of copays for medication, office visits, and other standard medical expenses, the situation seemed under control. When I find myself in a small financial crisis, I remember the story of Amaziah, a biblical king of Israel. He had spent a large sum of money to hire additional military support, and a "man of God" told him to release the troops (2 Chronicles 25:7–8). As his first concern, he questioned, "What shall we do about the hundred talents that I have given to the army of Israel?" (2 Chronicles 25:9). The response is a promise that I have taken to heart and personally experienced many times over in my life: "The Lord is able to give you much more than this" (2 Chronicles 25:9).

I have frequently found that when people have said that the Lord will provide, He does it in multiple ways. He will often minimize our expenditures, as in the case of us finding a surgeon covered by our insurance. Other times, He will bring an overwhelming sense of peace in knowing that whatever money has been "lost" is of no concern because He is able to provide in ways that we cannot even imagine. On rarer occasions, I have personally found that God will actually meet a financial need by providing additional sources of income. Such was the case on the first day of my family leave.

I came home from my last day of work on that Friday and saw that I had received a private message from a friend's mom on Facebook. Another time, several years ago, the mother of a friend from high school had reached out to our family after seeing pictures of our family on her daughter's account. She worked with a talent agency and had contacted us to suggest that we try to get Maggie, then an infant, into modeling. It is true that our daughter is the most beautiful girl in the world (just a slightly biased opinion). But, after hearing about the hours and hours and hours of time that we would have to spend traveling back and forth to New York City and the amount of commitment for something that we were not really keen on, we dismissed the thought and kept our beautiful daughter all to ourselves.

The message this day, however, was actually regarding an opportunity for me. My friend's mom knew that I worked as a nurse, and her agency was looking for healthcare workers who would be willing to submit photos for a McDonald's commercial. McDonald's was making a commercial to honor healthcare workers and celebrate their "Hero Meals," which they generously offered at no charge to healthcare workers. I told her about our son's upcoming surgery and said we really would not have the time to travel back and forth into the city. She informed me that all I had to do was fill out some papers and send in a few photos of me in my scrubs eating a Hero Meal. I reluctantly agreed, understanding that it was quite possible I could go through the entire process and not be selected.

Juli had never really wanted us to spend too much time eating fast food, but now, I had two reasons: I could get a free meal, and potentially, I could have a job with just a quick trip through the drive-through. So, I headed down the road with my cell phone in hand, ready to get this gig. After grabbing a few photos in the drive-through and then in the parking lot, I drove home to eat my free meal. I submitted the photos after spending a few hours completing the application, not expecting anything to come of it. A few weeks went by, and then, I heard back that my photos had been accepted for the commercial. I was shocked, but I still think the fact that half of my face was covered with a mask enabled them to look past my imperfections. I thoroughly enjoyed my 0.22 seconds of fame (https://www.youtube.com/watch?v=rkp_I-xJN2g), but I was even more grateful for the extra cash that would help with some of our family's additional medical bills. After the first check came in the mail, I was glad that I had been encouraged to go through with sending the photos in. How pleasantly surprised we were when two more checks came in the mail months later. Before the medical bills even started coming, we were comforted by the reality that our "God would supply all [our] need according to His riches in glory by Christ Jesus" (Philippians 4:19).

Refinancing

Yet there shall be a space between you and [the ark], about two thousand cubits by measure.
Do not come near it, that you may know the way by which you must go,
for you have not passed this way before.
Joshua 3:4

The fear and uncertainty we had about our ability to afford the potential medical bills were dismissed after seeing God provide through my "acting" gig. We knew God could surprise us, but we also knew that we should be wise stewards in how we handled the finances He blessed us with. We knew that we had an opportunity to minimize our monthly expenditures. One of my goals to accomplish during my family leave was to refinance our mortgage. Having never done this before, I knew I had a bit of homework ahead of me.

I spoke with family and friends who had gone through the process before and some who were actually in the middle of it. I probably would have been better off if I had found a mortgage broker to do the homework for me, but since I had some extra time at home, I began calling various lenders to see what we could find. After hours and days on the phone, we found a lender who was able to drop our interest rate by an entire percent. We were ultimately able to cut our monthly payment by approximately $100 and take the equivalent of two years (24 payments) off our mortgage. With other competing priorities taking up real estate in my mind, I would still not be the best person to ask about the refinancing process, but it all worked out. We completed the entire process over the phone and online. However, when our signatures were needed, the lender emphasized their "personal" touch by sending a representative to our home. Due to the length of the process and the date by which we needed to finalize the deal to lock in our rate, I was actually already in New Brunswick with August following one of his surgeries, which required an overnight stay. The lender drove to our house for my wife's signature and then, was fully prepared to make the hour-long drive to the hospital to meet me in the lobby for my signatures. We worked it out so my wife and I switched spots, and I was able to meet with the representative late that evening to close the deal.

We were getting quite good at this juggling act. Each of our other kids did not consume as much time as August in their early years, and now, we had more appointments and hospital visits than we ever had before in such a short span. So far this was a year of many firsts. We traveled down many roads in 2020 that we had never even looked at on our life map: our first refinance, our first major surgery for a child, our first overnight stay in a hospital for anyone in our family—all during our very first pandemic. And the fun was just beginning.

THE ADVENTURE BEGINS

The rest of this story will focus on what we faced for the remainder of the year. Our primary focus during this stage of life was maintaining August's kidney and bladder function. Many loved ones were praying for us and asking for updates, so I wrote and posted updates on social media. Most of what will be shared here regarding August's health will be those social media posts. I thought it best to share these posts since these reflections were written during the actual events. Interspersed throughout these updates, I will share some of the other major (and minor) events we squeezed in between August's medical appointments and surgeries. I hope that these "dated" posts will be better able to capture what our family was feeling and dealing with at the time.

August's Radiology Visits & Surgeries

2/29/2020 – US kidneys/bladder – identified bilateral duplicated collecting system; hydronephrosis in both kidneys

3/13/2020 – VCUG – large ureterocele; no reflux

4/23/2020 – US kidneys/bladder – large right ureterocele; severe hydronephrosis in the right kidney; worsening hydronephrosis in the left kidney

5/11/2020 – Surgery #1 – right ureterocele repair

5/27/2020 – Persistent large right ureterocele; worsening hydronephrosis in the right kidney; improved hydronephrosis in the left kidney but worsening left ureterectasis

6/3/2020 – Surgery #2 – bilateral nephrostomy tubes

6/9/2020 – Surgery #3 – unblock bilateral ureters; nephrostomy tubes still in place

6/16/2020 – Surgery #4 – stent placement (x2) in left ureter

7/10/2020 – US kidneys/bladder – severe hydronephrosis in bilateral kidneys with bilateral ureterectasis; bilateral ureteral stents in place; bladder severely distended with persistent, yet smaller ureterocele; sent to emergency department

7/20/2020 – US kidneys/bladder – improved hydronephrosis both kidneys. VCUG – bilateral vesicoureteral reflux; left greater than right

7/24/2020 – Surgery #5 – vesicostomy and ureter stent removal

8/14/2020 – US kidneys/bladder – worsening hydronephrosis bilaterally; ureteral stents removed; thickened wall in bladder

10/6/2020 – US kidneys/bladder – improved hydronephrosis and ureterectasis bilaterally; status post vesicostomy

11/9/2020 – US kidneys/bladder & VCUG (New Brunswick) – prior to admission to children's hospital for final surgery

11/23/2020 – Surgery #6 – vesicostomy reversal with left ureter detour, stents and right upper pole heminephrectomy

1/15/2021 – Surgery #7 – left ureter stent removal

First Surgery (May 11, 2020)
Right Ureterocele Repair (Outpatient)

Social Media Post

There's a classic Easter song from 1971 that has me thinking about this morning:

"How sweet to hold a newborn baby,
And feel the pride and joy he gives;
But greater still the calm assurance:
This child can face uncertain days because He lives!"

In the middle of this pandemic, many people have been going through some tough times. Not everyone's struggles are the same, and my heart goes out to all who have lost loved ones, suffered tremendously, or have been affected by this virus in one way or another. May we remember to consider the fact that this time has been more challenging for some and remember to pray for one another.

Our little August just went in for surgery this morning, and I was struck by the fact that due to the timing of my influenza A (missed August's birth, but thank you, Jennifer Montero, for saving the day!) and my self-quarantining due to my potential exposure to COVID-19 at the hospital (thank you, Malcolm and Joann Skelton, for saving the month!), I had not held August for more than five minutes until today, as we waited for him to go into surgery. This is a fairly minor procedure on his bladder that we knew he had to have since birth, but it has caused me to reconsider those lyrics. It was indeed sweet to hold my two-month-old son today for what I felt to be the first time, but "greater still the calm assurance, this child can face uncertain days because He lives." How fitting the chorus is during these uncertain times:

"Because He lives, I can face tomorrow,
Because He lives, all fear is gone;
Because I know He holds the future,
And life is worth the living,
Just because He lives!"
(Bill and Gloria Gaither, "Because He Lives," 2001)

Ultimately, my faith in my Savior Jesus Christ, who loved me and gave Himself for me, has given me hope during these times of hopelessness. He has given me peace in these times of restlessness. He has given me joy in this time of sorrow. I am so grateful for the salvation and forgiveness of sins that I have through the death and resurrection of my Savior. Thank you all so much for the prayers and love that have been poured out on August's behalf. We will keep you posted.

UPDATE: Surgery went well; nothing that wasn't expected. August has recovered, and we are on our way home! Thanks again for your prayers.

Homeschool

Train up a child in the way he should go, and when he is old he will not depart from it.
Proverbs 22:6

One of the many changes during the pandemic was the format of our daughter's education. Juli and I had discussed and prayed over the decision of whether to home-school our kids or have them attend public school. When Maggie was ready to start kindergarten, we settled on public school for a variety of reasons. That's another subject for another time, but ultimately, we concluded that each year we would reevaluate the situation and attempt to make the best decision. Over the years, as we discussed the possibility of home schooling, we were directed to a variety of resources. I appreciated the thoughts of authors David and Kelli Pritchard in their book *Going Public*. The author and his wife had decided to send their kids to public school, but when asked if they home-school their children, they respond, "Of course, we home-school our children. They spend a few hours a day in public school, but yes, we home-school them." The lesson for me was that a child's education does not start and stop at the sound of the school bell. As a parent, I have the responsibility to constantly teach my children at home, no matter where their formal education takes place.

Maggie started her kindergarten school year in our town's public school system, but after one week of school cancellation, all students were forced to go virtual. It looked like we were going to be home-schooling whether we wanted to or not. The school provided real-time learning sessions as well as self-directed learning activities. It was far from perfect, but we understood the challenges considering the sudden nature of the virtual format. This gave us a glimpse of what the home-school atmosphere would be like. We were grateful that Juli had been able to stay home with the kids in recent years, so the transition was doable for us. Many other families with single parents or homes where both parents were working full-time jobs had extreme difficulty in coordinating their kids' school schedule with their work schedule.

We spoke with many friends and family members as we ventured through this partial year of virtual learning. In my arrogance, I told Juli that we could easily teach Maggie in a more efficient and effective way. Parents we knew who had home-schooled their children shared their insight into customizing materials to develop a personalized curriculum that works best for each kid. This was always in the back of our mind, but a unique opportunity came up that gave us more insight into the home-schooling world.

A friend of ours, Kim, who shared her experiences of home schooling all three of her children, had reached out to ask me to share some challenging thoughts at their homeschool co-op graduation ceremony. I was more than willing to do it, but having never home-schooled before, I felt completely unqualified for the job. Kim and I spoke about how their co-op had run for years (in which she was deeply involved), which provided me with more insight into what to share and future decisions for our own family. The conversations I had with Kim led me to share what had been on my mind for the last few months. The overwhelming sense of division across the country over many topics was an issue that I felt had to be addressed for these graduates. For all high school graduates, 2020 was quite an unusual year to finish twelfth grade. These young men and women were about to head into a world ravaged by division, turmoil, and confrontation. The ceremony was indeed an eye-opening experience and it proved very insightful as Juli and I were considering the possibility of home-schooling our daughter for the upcoming school year.

I shared the following address with those graduates, and I believe there are many applicable truths to help all of us at this point in time in our nation's history:

"Good morning, graduates, parents, family, and friends. Thank you so much for this opportunity and privilege to join with you in celebrating the 2020 graduates! I would like to take a few moments this morning to consider unity and diversity.

I was asked to keep it brief, but when I heard that the ceremony was not going to be outside in the heat but in the comfort of an air-conditioned building, I decided to take some time to make this a little more interactive. Just to show how diverse we are, by show of hands, how many of you: Are an only child vs. have siblings, oldest vs. youngest; consider yourself conservative vs. liberal, submissive vs. rebellious, straight-A student vs. straight whatever the bare minimum grade that's required to pass? No matter the path, you all made it here. You were not alone. Your loved ones helped you make it this far. But you're not here simply because of *their* choices. Yes, their decisions helped guide you, but you ultimately chose to put the time in, put the hard work in, and by the grace of God, here we are. We have different households, various upbringings, unique life experiences, but they brought us to this same point in time. Different paths brought us to this one room at this singular moment in time for this one purpose: to celebrate your achievement of graduating high school, and when we leave this moment of solidarity, we will all take different paths. Some of you may enter the workforce, go to trade school, attend community college, public or private university, Christian or secular.

The decisions you make may lead you in *different* directions, but don't let them ever *divide* you! Don't let your diversity lead you to division!

We live in the United States of America—I repeat, the *United* States of America—and yet I have never seen this country so divided.

I want to take a few moments to consider the importance of unity. Unity, more than ever, is crucial at this time in our nation's history—not just unity as Americans, but as disciples, as followers, as imitators of our Lord Jesus Christ. This country has been divided in so many ways in recent months. We are divided politically, we are divided racially, and we have become divided spiritually. It has become Republican vs. Democrat, White vs. Black, home school vs. public school, vaxxers vs. antivaxxers, those who wear masks vs. those who don't, Christ follower vs. Christ follower. I wish I didn't have to list that last one. I really wish I didn't have to list any of them.

Yet, as I just mentioned, we have become so divided over so many things. Herein lies the problem: It's not that we shouldn't discuss issues of politics or health or race; the problem is that we do not have the goal of unity in mind. People are looking for opportunities to cause division. Let's briefly look at two specific examples: the COVID-19 crisis and race relations.

Considering recent conversations around the COVID-19 pandemic, I have personally seen friends driven apart over whether or not to wear a mask. Family members stop speaking to one another because of differing opinions on whether or not to get the vaccine if or when they develop one. Small business owners and healthcare workers debate if businesses should open up. Church leaders close their doors temporarily because of disagreements of how or when to physically regather.

To pursue unity, we must listen. As a healthcare worker, I have seen young, healthy coworkers, friends of mine, suffer from strokes related to COVID-19. I have seen patients who were unable to have their families with them as they took their last breath. I have had friends who have lost loved ones due to the virus. Personally, I was ready to say, "Take every precaution necessary. Don't open up businesses yet." But I am not a small business owner. My brother runs a small bike shop. It's easy from *my* perspective to say, "Don't stay open." But my income has not been affected. My ability to provide for my family has remained intact. To pursue unity even within my own family, I must take on the mind of Christ and esteem others better than myself (Philippians 2:3). What is it like to be a husband and a father and not be able to provide for my family? I must be able to share my experiences while willingly and lovingly listening to the experiences of others.

To pursue unity, we must listen. When considering race relations, I needed to realize that racism is a much bigger problem in America today than I had initially thought. As personally never having been a victim of blatant or even subtle racist attacks, I needed to speak to individuals with diverse backgrounds who could reveal what *they* had personally experienced. If we are not willing to listen, we're not really pursuing unity. In the past few weeks, I have seen childhood friends who grew up together send vicious attacks to one another—things that I don't even feel comfortable repeating—over social media while "discussing" the problem of racism. And this is between two followers of Christ! In the Holy Spirit-inspired words of James, "Brothers and sisters, these things ought not to be so" (James 3:10).

Diversity should not equal division.

Some of you may be going to a university when you graduate. I graduated with my Bachelor of Science in Nursing from Messiah College, and in fact, in just four days, they are officially changing the name to Messiah University. There is debate over where this word originated and what it actually means. Some say it means "the whole truth" in early Latin. As a major side note, it's important to note that while this morning we are focused on achieving unity, we want to be sure to never forsake the truth simply for the sake of unity. Some say it means a "community of scholars" in late Latin. Many others have shared the more modern sentiment that *university* means "unity in diversity."

When I chose to go to Messiah College, some older saints told me that I was making the wrong choice: "How can you be a light in a dark world if you are enclosing yourself in that 'Christian bubble'?" The world we live in is in desperate need of the gospel and in dire need of real biblical truth, but trust me, you can be a light on a Christian campus. You can be light on a secular campus, at a community college, at your job.

But the one thing that I appreciated the most about attending Messiah College was that I was faced with new and sometimes challenging interpretations of the Word of God that differed from what I learned growing up. This caused me to question what I believed in a good way. My faith was slowly transforming from something that I believed because that's what my home church taught me into something I believe because I have searched the Scriptures myself and allowed the Holy Spirit to provide discernment. My faith became more real to me—not because I was able to yell louder than those who had opposing views, but because we listened to each other. We had conversations about biblical passages and how they could be interpreted and how that should shape our worldviews. Was there diversity that sometimes caused division? Absolutely. But I thank God for the diversity that led to those tough conversations that, in fact, brought unity among brothers and sisters in Christ and, in turn, strengthened my faith.

Diversity causing division is not a new problem. In every single one of Paul's epistles addressed to local churches, Paul expresses a desire for unity. He calls out individuals and groups of believers for not seeking unity in their common faith in the Lord Jesus Christ. He commands them to make this a priority as they gather together:

- "Be of one mind and live in peace" (2 Corinthians 3:11).
- "There is neither Jew nor Greek, there is neither slave nor free, there is neither male nor female; for you are all one in Christ" (Gal. 3:28).
- "That you may stand fast in one spirit, with one mind striving together for the faith of the gospel" (Philippians 1:27).
- "Bearing with one another in love, endeavoring to keep the unity of the Spirit in the bond of peace. There is one body and one Spirit, just as you were called in one hope of your calling, one Lord, one faith, one baptism; one God and Father of all" (Ephesians 4:26).

Jesus Christ Himself, on His way to the cross, in His prayer to the Father in the garden, revealed a heart that clearly longed for unity among His followers. Here He is, the Son of God, at what many would call His darkest hour, and He not only prays for His disciples but look where His thoughts turn: "I do not pray for these alone, but also for those who will believe in Me through their word" (John 17:20). He's praying for you and for me! And what does He pray for specifically? As we read in the very next verse, He prays "that they all may be one, as You, Father, are in Me, and I in You; that they also may be one in Us, that the world may believe that You sent Me." His prayer is for unity among believers and unity for believers with Himself and the Father." What's the purpose of this unity among ourselves and unity with the Godhead? That the world may believe!

The world will believe that Jesus is the Son of God who loved them and gave His life for them by our unity! To the graduates, as you take different steps in different directions towards different goals, don't let your diversity divide you. Don't hide your Lord and Savior from the world by biting and devouring one another, as the apostle Paul instructs the Galatians (Galatians 5:15).

We read this in Romans 15:5–7: "Now may the God of patience and comfort grant you to be like-minded toward one another, according to Christ Jesus, that you may with one mind and one mouth glorify the God and Father of our Lord Jesus Christ. Therefore receive one another, just as Christ also received us, to the glory of God."

We close with one final thought. There was a tremendously difficult time in the history of the nation of Israel when they returned home after living as exiles in a foreign land. As they came together to hear the Word of God, we learn a valuable lesson from them concerning unity. "All the people gathered together as *one man* and were attentive to the Book of the Law" (Nehemiah 8:1, 3). That was their time, but what does it have to do with the graduating class of 2020? I challenge you with this: This is your time. Gather together as one man, unified in purpose, and listen attentively. May you journey on, pursuing unity in the midst of diversity. Thank you."

Navigating the System

The expectation following our son's first ureterocele repair was that August's ureter would be able to drain urine from the kidney into the bladder. The delay in surgery caused by the COVID-19 pandemic resulted in damage to the upper pole of his right kidney and a stiffening of the bladder wall. The partial loss of kidney function was not a concern for August's urologist as he was confident that he would be fine with a good one-and-a-half kidneys. The bladder wall stiffening resulted from the bladder's inability to fill and empty regularly. We were told that this may delay potty training but that August should recover fully. We were thrilled to hear that all had gone well, meaning August would not need to stay overnight for observation, and the plan was August would have periodic ultrasounds to ensure that the kidneys were draining. All the while, August would continue his prophylactic dose of antibiotics until his first birthday.

As we waited for his next ultrasound appointment, we kept an eye out for any fevers or other signs of infection. Thankfully, no fevers came.

The good news about the amount of follow-up we had to do was that most of it could be completed five minutes down the road at the hospital where I worked. After speaking with Dr. Barone, he shared with me that Monmouth Medical Center was a part of the University Radiology group and that all of August's images would be available immediately following his exams since they would be uploaded to a database. This news was great since we did not want to delay any interventions for our son. Following one of his ultrasounds, we asked the MMC radiology department if the images would be uploaded to the database. We were informed that the department had recently made the transition to University Radiology and they were not yet able to upload images.

I will be the first to confess that I have no idea how to interpret ultrasound imaging or even interpret the radiologist's interpretation. However, as I read the summary, my heart sank every time I came across the words *worsening* or *increased hydronephrosis* or *no improvement from previous study*. I felt hopeless. I felt like all of the efforts up until this point had been a waste of time. I was frustrated and even angry that the first surgery had not improved little Augie's situation. Due to MMC Radiology's recent transition, I knew we had to find another way of getting the images to Dr. Barone. The staff at MMC told me that I would have to sign a release form, which would have to get faxed to the doctor's office. The office staff would then have to send a release form back to MMC, which I would have to sign and send back to them. Then, once MMC confirmed that they had received the completed form, they would be allowed to send the discs up to Dr. Barone. The next ultrasound was scheduled for a Monday. I found out that the images would have to be delivered on a Wednesday. I started the consent form process on the Thursday before but realized that the multiple correspondences necessary would never be completed by Friday. The hospital had to send their packages via FedEx mail, and if I were lucky and they were able to send the release form before the close of business on that Friday, it still might take anywhere from five to seven days to arrive.

For the sake of my son, I felt as if this were an unacceptable amount of time for images to be delivered. Having worked in healthcare, I understood that certain protocols must be followed, but being on the patient side of things infuriated me. It was unbelievable that if only MMC had transitioned to the new radiology group a few weeks earlier, the urologist would be able to see the images in a matter of minutes. However, the ongoing transition was now going to delay any interventions that were necessary for my son.

When I received the call that the process would most likely hinder the images from getting to New Brunswick as late as the middle of next week, I decided to take matters into my own hands. I was on a walk with August a few blocks from our house at 4 o'clock in the afternoon. I had another one of the kids riding their bike alongside me. I determined in my heart and mind that these images would get up to New Brunswick that day. I would have been able to enjoy the beautiful afternoon sunshine if I had not had to cut through a cemetery, running at full speed while pushing a stroller with a kid on a bike behind me to get back to my house.

By the time I left the house, it was 4:25 p.m. When I spoke to the office, they said that they closed at 5:00 p.m. Our drive to New Brunswick typically takes anywhere from 45 minutes to over an hour. I made it up to the office in record time. I parked illegally in the front of the building to run the images up at 4:55 p.m. This was my son, and I was not going to sit back and wait while he needed further intervention.

Unfortunately, the result of his follow-up ultrasound did indeed show worsening hydronephrosis. The ureterocele repair was not successful, and urine was still backing up in the kidney. The disappointment and frustration were overwhelming. We had been forced to wait this long for his corrective surgery, and now, we were told that our son had to go back in for a second surgery.

This news did not come in the most convenient fashion (as bad news typically does). I was at an eye appointment when I received the call from the urologist, early in the week following the ultrasound. He said that he had gotten a chance to review the images, and the hydronephrosis had gotten so severe that I should head up to the New Brunswick emergency department that evening so August could be admitted for surgery the next morning.

I never worked in an emergency department, but I had spent plenty of time there during my nursing education career. We were still only a few months into the COVID-19 pandemic, and some of the things I had witnessed in the past few months seemed surreal, like a scene out of a movie. However, our experience there was far from scary. August was not allowed to eat after midnight, due to the planned surgery. Despite the doctor's plans for an early morning procedure, August did not go down until 1:00 p.m., and for a four-month-old to not eat for so long, I knew this would be difficult. I know that it was only by the grace of God that August did not cry once that entire morning. Oftentimes, it's the little things in life that cause you to pause and be grateful in the unimaginable circumstances.

Second Surgery (June 3, 2020)
Bilateral Nephrostomy Tubes

Social Media Post

Round Two: August's procedure three weeks ago did not resolve his issue, so we are back at the hospital awaiting the placement of bilateral nephrostomy tubes this morning and diagnostic testing to see what our next steps need to be. Seems like more questions than answers at this point in time, but as I sat by the window of August's hospital room and heard the thunder and watched the rain and lightning last night, I was reminded of an old song by Casting Crowns:

> *I'll praise You in this storm*
> *And I will lift my hands*
> *For You are who You are*
> *No matter where I am*
> *And every tear I've cried*
> *You hold in Your hand*
> *You never left my side*
> *And though my heart is torn*
> *I will praise You in this storm.*
> (Bernie Herms and John Mark Hall, "Praise You in The Storm," 2005)

I'm so thankful for the "God of all comfort, who comforts us in all of our tribulation" (2 Corinthians 1:3). Thank you all for your prayers. We will keep you posted.

Update: August did well during the procedure. The doctor was able to determine there is a blockage in right upper ureter leading to upper lobe of kidney and blockage in left ureter. Two tests tomorrow and possible plan for Monday...Surgical removal of right upper ureter and right upper portion of kidney is planned (if not functioning) and disconnect, remove blockage, and reconnect the left ureter. Thanks for your prayers.

Church Life

Besides these other things, what comes upon me daily: my deep concern for all the churches.
2 Corinthians 11:28

Similar to the school year, our local church halted its services for a brief time before resuming virtually. This was a new adventure for us since we had never had much of an online presence since Fifth Avenue Chapel opened its doors many decades ago. In one sense, the COVID-19 pandemic forced us to move ahead in a direction that we perhaps needed to go. Since my in-laws were helping at home with August, and I was "stranded" at my five-star hotel with perfectly good internet access and minimal responsibilities outside of work, I became the "tech crew" for our small congregation. By *tech crew*, I mean I had to spend a few afternoons learning about Zoom, creating an account, and familiarizing myself with some of its features.

The first few meetings felt like a disaster as I tried to ensure that it all ran smoothly. I had never sweat so much during a church service. The biggest challenge was keeping an eye on the large number of those logged on who appeared as if they had never used a computer before (my parents included). It was interesting to note that those who claimed that they did not know how to mute themselves could somehow always find a way to unmute themselves immediately after I took the liberty to mute them. Eventually, most people learned to manage their audio and video controls, and the Zoom services flowed much more smoothly.

The format for our services obviously changed drastically. Much of our gatherings were dependent on physically being together. Acts 2:42 provides an example as the early Christians "continued steadfastly in the apostles' doctrine and fellowship, in the breaking of bread, and in prayers." The doctrine piece was simple enough to continue as our speaker each Sunday morning was given Zoom's "host" privileges and shared from the Word. Our midweek prayer meeting continued with slight adjustments. The challenges came with continuing steadfastly in fellowship and the breaking of bread.

Fellowship, or the mutual sharing, participation, and encouragement in the Christian faith, was meant to take place in person. The status of the COVID-19 situation caused us to learn to make use of Zoom's breakout rooms and do the best we could. The Breaking of Bread, or communion service, was a bit of a challenge as well. The structure for this remembrance meeting is an open-format in which various men share a thought, pray, read a Bible passage, or request to sing a hymn all for the purpose of remembering the Lord Jesus Christ and His sacrifice for our sins on the cross at Calvary. This meeting is a celebration of our salvation through faith alone in Christ and a "time of refreshing that comes from the presence of the Lord" (Ephesians 2:8; Acts 3:20). A major component is the partaking of the bread and the cup, which, biblically, was practiced while members of the early church were physically together. While not ideal, we learned how to make the best of our current situation and gather in remembrance of our Savior's sacrifice virtually. We moved toward a more structured format along with a time for open sharing for the sake of order while we learned the many nuances of Zoom.

Shortly after the first few weeks, a number of other men had jumped in to share responsibilities in facilitating the Zoom meetings, for which I was incredibly grateful. Long conversations and in-depth discussions would take place over the next few months as we planned our steps to rejoin in-person and gather in a wise and profitable manner. After a few months' break, we went back to meeting in-person with a virtual option. Almost a year later, the method of our gathering would continue to be a topic of conversation as we prayerfully considered how to progress.

We had heard of religious gatherings struggling through the pandemic and some meetings even shutting their doors. While the perspectives and opinions on how to handle the pandemic precautions varied greatly even within our own assembly, we thank God for the grace and patience that our chapel family expressed toward one another. The struggle continued as we attempted to navigate the ever-changing precautions and recommendations as the pandemic developed. The leadership at our assembly knew that this would be an ongoing journey for an indefinite amount of time, so we trusted in the One who knew how it would all play out.

Third Surgery (June 9, 2020)
Unblock Bilateral Ureters

Social Media Post

Round Three: August just went back for his five- to six-hour surgery to remove a portion of his right kidney that is no longer functioning and to unblock his left ureter (tube from kidney to bladder). The surgeon is optimistic that if all goes well, he will have normal kidney function. He will stay for a few days which will allow them to remove his nephrostomy tubes after monitoring him post-surgery. We will keep you posted. Thank you once again for your prayers.

On my drive to the hospital this morning, I felt as if God had a message specifically for me. I was listening to a preacher on the radio who gave this challenge: "How does your prayer life change when you are faced with challenges?"

Gratitude. First off, it caused me to consider how appreciative our family is of the prayers and encouragement from all of our friends and family during August's health issues. We are overwhelmed by the expressions of love and concern poured out on our family. Thank you.

Conviction. I confess that my prayer life often changes drastically when I face trials. For all of the God-believing, God-fearing individuals out there, God desires for His people to turn to Him in prayer and even requests it (2 Chronicles 7:14; Proverbs 15:8). But, often, when life is going well, my prayer life is extremely lacking. I turn from dependence on God to dependence on self—how I can meet my needs—because things have not (from my prideful perspective) gotten beyond my control. During this difficult time, I realize that things are beyond my control, and it forces me to depend on a sovereign God who is in control. What a great place to be. Unfortunately, it is a place I should constantly be at according to 1 Thessalonians 5:16–18: "Rejoice always, pray without ceasing, give thanks in all circumstances; for this is the will of God in Christ Jesus for you." May we continually seek His face in any and every circumstance.

Action. My prayer life is usually affected the most when I am personally impacted by something. In August's case, *my* health is not really affected at all, but my prayer life has changed because of the impact on the well-being of my son, someone whom I care for and love deeply. What if all of us prayed as if we were personally impacted by every hardship of our friends and family? I am reminded by recent events that this is a critical time in our country to pray. Why? Although I may not fully understand how all of my loved ones are suffering, each of them is experiencing some sort of hardship that is deeply personal. Romans 12:15 commands us to "rejoice with those who rejoice, weep with those who weep." Many of my friends and family have been hurt by recent events, whether by social injustices experienced over a lifetime, recent health crises caused by the pandemic, or something that grieves a loved one so much that only that individual can express how painful the experience has been. May we continually offer up prayers to God for the pain that they are experiencing, but may it lead us to action.

When I heard that August needed surgery, if I had decided to sit at home and say, "Let me just pray that God takes it away," but not act on that prayer, would that have pleased God? While I believe that God is fully capable of miraculously healing my son, I also believe that He has provided us with skilled caregivers whom He can use to bring about that healing.

I can pray, and I can act.

While I believe that God can bring healing to this nation, do I believe that God is perhaps calling me to action, to show the love of Jesus Christ to those who are suffering? While I can't fully understand each person's suffering, am I willing to listen, learn, weep with those who weep, and ask God how I can be used for His glory?

We can pray, and we can act.

It is evident that we live in a broken world. Sin in the human heart is the cause of all of this suffering. Romans 5:12 tells us that death and suffering came into the world through sin. And I share with you personally where I have found my peace, where I have found my hope, and where I have found the forgiveness of my sins, which is offered to all who believe: "But God demonstrates His own love toward us, in that while we were still sinners, Christ died for us. Much more then, having now been justified by His blood, we shall be saved from wrath through Him. For if when we were enemies we were reconciled to God through the death of His Son, much more, having been reconciled, we shall be saved by His life. And not only that, but we also rejoice in God through our Lord Jesus Christ, through whom we have now received the reconciliation" (Romans 5:8–11).
Love you all.

Update: The surgery went well. Some challenges once they got in there, but they were able to resolve the blockage issues on both sides without removing any part of the right kidney. Nephrostomy tubes still temporarily in place and monitoring for next two days. Thank you for your prayers.

Fourth Surgery (June 16, 2020)
Stent Placement (x2) in Left Ureter

Social Media Post

Round Four: August goes for a study this morning at 8:00 a.m. to see why he still has some blockage in the left ureter. He will be sedated, and they plan on inserting a stent to keep the urine flowing from the left kidney down to the bladder. It has been a long and exhausting week, but we thank God for His preservation of most of August's kidney function and for the great care that we have received. Thank you all for your prayers and encouragement through all of this. We will keep you updated.

Update: The procedure was successful! Two stents were placed side by side in the lower left ureter due to how "twisty" it was (that's the official medical terminology). We are in the recovery room now and August will have to be monitored for a few days to make sure there's no leakage from the nephrostomy and more urine goes into his diaper. Thanks again so much for your prayers.

A Not-So-Brief History on August

The mind of man plans his way, But the Lord directs his steps.
Proverbs 16:9

Social Media Post (June 20, 2020)

August was discharged from the hospital this past Thursday after what felt like a long 10 days of surgeries, procedures, tests, and blood work. Thank you all once again for your prayers and words of encouragement.

As I reflect on the past few months, the verse above has played out in my mind and in our lives like we have never seen. When we found out that our soon-to-be-born son was going to need a consult with a pediatric urologist, we immediately got in touch with a well-respected group in our area.

Our plan #1: After our first visit, we were told that August would need a simple surgery to correct his problem, but that very same day was when all of the local hospitals began to cancel all of their "elective" surgeries due to the COVID-19 pandemic and its impact on our local region. August's issue was more of an urgent one but was not considered emergent, so his surgery was delayed more than two months. In finding that he lost part of the function of his right kidney due to the delay, we were more than upset. This was not part of the plan we had in mind, but God had a better plan.

Our plan #2: We chose our pediatric urologist based on their ability to perform surgeries at the hospital where I worked. However, by the time our pediatric urologist was allowed to perform August's surgery, the pediatric unit had been converted to an adult ICU for COVID-19 patients, and August could not have his surgery performed there. August's doctor was only able to schedule him at another local hospital that was out of our health insurance network. Despite the extenuating circumstances, when I spoke with our insurance, we were told that to have his surgery at this other hospital, we would potentially pay over $10,000 out of pocket. We were more than upset about this. This was not part of the plan we had in mind, but God had a better plan.

Our plan #3: While we could never put a price on the health and well-being of our son, we were desperate to see if August's issue could be resolved in-network. We were able to get an appointment with another highly recommended pediatric urologist at an in-network hospital 45 minutes away. The appointment was actually on the same day as his otherwise scheduled procedure, so we rescheduled his surgery for a later date at this in-network hospital. On May 11, August had his first surgery to correct his urinary issue. All seemed to go well, but the follow-up ultrasound showed worsening kidney issues. We were more than upset about this. This was not part of the plan we had in mind, but God had a better plan.

God's plan #1: We were told to go to the emergency department on June 2 as soon as our pediatric urologist saw the ultrasound images. August had two nephrostomy tubes implanted the next morning. While traveling through the hallways of this children's hospital, I kept seeing signs highlighting the hospital's various programs. It turns out that the pediatric urology program at this particular facility was ranked by U.S. News & World Report as the best program in the state and the 38th best in the country. When we found out about the complexity of August's issues, we knew that God had orchestrated the details, the disappointments, and the direction of our plans to get us exactly where we needed to be. Not only was the surgery going to be covered by our insurance (the least of our worries), August also ended up with the best pediatric urologist in the state. We could never have even dreamed up a plan this good on our own! This was not part of the plan we had in mind, but God had a better plan.

God's plan #2: While the nephrostomy tubes were a temporary solution, August was discharged on Friday, June 5, only to return the following Tuesday, June 9, for his major surgery. When the surgeon went in, the anatomical anomalies were much different and more complex than they had initially believed. After more than six hours in the operating room, August's surgery was complete. I am not doubting the ability of our first pediatric urologist, but with our new doctor having more than 25 years of experience and over 700 surgeries per year, we knew that God had put our son in the care of the best individual around. We also knew the promise of Psalm 31:19, "How abundant are the good things that You have stored up for those who fear You, that You bestow in the sight of all, on those who take refuge in You." This was not part of the plan we had in mind, but God had a better plan.

God's plan #3: Despite all going well with the surgery, urine was not flowing from the kidney to the bladder when the left nephrostomy was capped. This extended our stay since August needed to have a stent inserted to help the urine go in the right direction. After a successful procedure, despite a few setbacks, August began to improve to the point where he was well enough to be discharged. This was not part of the plan we had in mind, but God had a better plan.

Throughout this entire ordeal, we realized that so many things did not go as we had planned, but we are so glad that this was the path God led us down. If left to our own decisions and wisdom, our plans would have left us with more problems than we could imagine, but when we allowed the Lord to direct our steps, God in His sovereignty brought everything together. There are so many other seemingly small details that confirmed God's hand in all of this, but we can safely say that all of these circumstances were not coincidences.

Was it easy for us to see all of our plans fall apart amid a pandemic? Not at all. Was it easy for us to see our son's health deteriorate and move from one complication to the next? Not at all. Was it amazing to see God work behind the scenes in bringing us exactly where we needed to be? Absolutely.

"And the peace of God, which transcends all understanding, will guard your hearts and your minds in Christ Jesus" (Philippians 4:7).

Unexpected

You would think that, after four "successful" surgeries, August would start to turn the corner and his ultrasounds would begin to improve. Unfortunately, we got some news that we were not expecting during his next visit to the radiology department on July 10. His hydronephrosis and ureterectasis (swelling and dilation of the ureters) were worse compared to his last ultrasound. Having been told how well his previous surgeries had gone, we were shocked. However, this was not the worst news. The ultrasound showed a distended bladder with 193 milliliters of urine. Now, I was not too concerned with this volume since I had been training staff on how to perform bladder scans for more than eight years. However, I had to be reminded that the bladder of a 5-month-old retaining 193 milliliters was not typical. In fact, after unsuccessfully attempting all sorts of tricks to get August to empty his bladder on his own, we were sent to the emergency department to get a catheter inserted.

We received great care in the ED, and after a fairly short time, a new urinary catheter was inserted, and August's bladder was relieved. We were surprised to notice that an indwelling catheter was placed without any sort of drainage bag. This was not the first time that we had seen August with a catheter that simply drained into his diaper. Each time, I had questioned this practice, having never worked with pediatric patients. It would never be done for an adult patient, and since our son was already at a higher risk for developing a UTI, I called everyone and their mother to ask if this was a common practice. My concern was that August would poop in his diaper, and the catheter would be contaminated. I was reassured from many sources that this practice was common. Time would tell if August would remain free from an infection. And sure enough, time told us.

Fever

I've got a fever, and the only prescription is more (nitrofurantoin).
Christopher Walken (sort of)

August began dealing with fevers on and off, so despite being on a low-dose prophylactic antibiotic since the day he was born, we had to start him on higher doses of different antibiotics whenever he began to develop fevers. On one such occasion, the treatment doses of the various antibiotics we had previously used no longer did the trick. So the urologist prescribed nitrofurantoin and recommended we start it the day of the fever to minimize any serious harm to August's kidneys. The challenge we faced was finding a pharmacy that could fill this prescription on short notice. Nitrofurantoin is not necessarily a difficult antibiotic to find, but to get it as an oral solution at the dosage prescribed was next to impossible. We called all of the big chain pharmacies that we had gone to before, and none of them had it. We asked them to check in their system, and they could not find a dose anywhere. Juli and I began to check some of the privately owned pharmacies with no success either. We eventually got in touch with a local retail pharmacy that gave us a glimmer of hope.

The staff told us that there was a dose in one of their pharmacies about half an hour away. When I called that pharmacy, they confirmed they had it. However, I learned that this medication, which would have cost me a $5 copay at Walgreens if in stock, would cost me over $250 at this pharmacy. It seemed outrageous that I would have to pay so much more for the same antibiotic at a retail pharmacy that did not fall under my insurance plan, but as I have already mentioned, navigating the insurance world is not my forte. However, I can now share one trick: if you are ever in a situation where your medication is not covered by insurance, simply ask if they have any sort of "discount" available. If you work with the right pharmacist, he or she may even suggest said discount without your inquiring. Such was the case with this liquid gold. A seemingly random discount brought the price down to $115. Part of me was hesitant, reluctant even, to pay a hefty price tag for such a small bottle, but the urologist was emphatic that we start the doses that night if we wanted to avoid hospitalization.

If you see oral-solution nitrofurantoin, you might guess that it is not the most delightful medicine to taste. If you have ever seen the 1991 classic live-action film *Teenage Mutant Ninja Turtles II: The Secret of the Ooze*, one of my favorite movies, this antibiotic looks like the ooze. And judging by August's reaction, it tastes like it too. I believe August had tried to start this exact medication during one of his previous UTIs, but due to his inability to tolerate the taste, the urologist switched it. Since we had tried so many other treatments and the UTIs kept coming back, we were told that nitrofurantoin would most likely be the best medication for him. We decided to mix the medication with some mashed-up bananas since August loved bananas. The special blend had barely even touched his lips when he began to projectile vomit. Not even kidding. I thought I ruined bananas for him for the rest of his life. My first thought was *what are we going to do to treat this UTI?* My second thought was *I just paid $115 for this junk!* My wife and I prayed, having no idea what to do and expecting we would need to bring August to the hospital at some point in the middle of the night.

We decided to take a break and revisit the antibiotic situation in a little bit. We were feeling hopeless and helpless. After struggling to determine our next steps and having mentally prepared for the undesirable trip to New Brunswick in the middle of the night, I remembered 2 Corinthians 12:9, where Paul reminds the church at Corinth of God's promise: "My grace is sufficient for you, for My power is made perfect in weakness. Therefore, I will boast all the more gladly of my weaknesses, so that the power of Christ may rest upon me." We needed God to remind us that in those moments when we feel the weakest, God has the best opportunity to reveal His strength to us. We tried to administer the dose of nitrofurantoin one tiny drop at a time, and despite August giving us the most disgusted face we had ever seen him make, he eventually tolerated it. We continued to give it little by little, and August seemed to mind it less and less. He eventually took it like a champ, and we were able to successfully treat the UTI. We must remember that when the situation appears out of our hands, we can take comfort in knowing that the situation is in His hands.

Support

As iron sharpens iron, so a friend sharpens a friend.
Proverbs 27:17

August recovered from this fever, but it was never easy to see him go through any of his UTIs. The hours immediately following each of his surgeries were always challenging, but the fevers made him feel so miserable. The added responsibilities of managing August's medications and nephrostomy tube sites as well as caring for his basic needs (and our other three kids) really took a toll on us. Little did we know that the management of his surgical sites would become exponentially more challenging. I believe it goes without saying (I would be at a fault for not actually saying it), but I cannot imagine how difficult all of this would have been without my wife. Juli was the hero in so many ways.

During August's earlier surgeries, Juli and I felt more comfortable with me staying at the bedside to help grasp all that was going on regarding his care. However, we found out rather quickly that August preferred his mommy at his side. During each of the hospital stays where I was with August and Juli was at home with the other kids, August's biggest struggle was feeding. Juli had breastfed August since the day he was born with little to no supplemental bottle feeding. So, the reality was that when we were in New Brunswick for an outpatient procedure or overnight for an inpatient stay, August had to learn to bottle feed on the spot, which he did—sort of. The first few times, he was so fussy, and I tried holding him in all sorts of positions and readjusting the bottle to no avail. I was actually quite surprised by how long August was able to go without eating, especially when he could not eat (NPO or "nothing by mouth") after midnight for some of his procedures that did not take place until as late as 2:00 p.m. I was successful on one occasion: I found that if I stood on his left side, slid my hand under his neck, gently rubbed his right cheek, placed the bottle at a slightly higher angle, and otherwise remained perfectly still with shallow breaths, I had success! Otherwise, he didn't eat well for me. So, we decided to switch places for his future surgeries. Despite Juli's attitude regarding hospitals (not to mention that we were on a unit with COVID-19 pediatric patients), she seemed better fit to stay with August and breastfeed him and I was better fit to take the big kids on hikes and bike rides.

The support in the hospital went beyond my wife. One experience with the urologist caused me to pause and be thankful for the nursing staff as well. I preface this by saying that, at this point, we had the utmost confidence in Dr. Barone since he had taken such great care of August so far. However, after one of his surgeries, Dr. Barone came up to Augie's room and had a puzzled look on his face. He inquired about a yellow stripe down the middle of our son's diaper that had started to turn blue. After explaining to him that this feature in diapers notifies parents that their child had urinated, I quickly called Juli and asked, "How long has this guy been in the urology business? How does he not know about the yellow-to-blue stripe on diapers?"

All kidding aside, we knew that our son was under the best care, from physicians and nurses alike. Oftentimes, following a sleepless night, the staff would come into the room and hold or feed August if he was restless or crying. I did not want to be "that dad" that the staff talked smack about at the nurses' station, but after being awake for more than 30 hours, I was incredibly appreciative of the staff. I also ran into a woman from a church that I had visited. She worked on the unit, and we had an encouraging conversation and prayed together.

I don't know how people go through many of life's trials without support from loved ones. I feel as if I would crack under the pressure. I have often experienced God reminding me of His presence and His provision through the people He has placed in my life. In addition to my family and my local church family, I cannot adequately express my gratitude for another group of people. A number of years ago, I reconnected with a few friends from high school. This group of guys had started to get together for a Bible study on a fairly regular basis. It was such an incredible experience to reconnect with these guys and not only spend time in the Word of God and in prayer but to also share our struggles. We would regularly encourage one another and live out Galatians 6:2 by "bearing one another's burdens" in the various family, work, and personal issues that each of us were battling at the time.

At one such meeting, we were in a friend's garage, and we decided to open up our time with a few songs. Soon after we started, I got a call from Juli informing me that August had come down with another really high fever. I was so frustrated that August kept getting these UTIs, and I will openly admit that I was frustrated with God. I thought we had done everything right in getting August the best care possible. Why wasn't God fixing this problem for us? As I re-entered the garage to let the guys know I had to leave, they were coming up to the chorus of the song below, and the words really hit me as exactly what I needed to hear at that time:

Way Maker, Miracle Worker
Promise Keeper, Light in the Darkness
My God, that is who You are.

Even when I don't see it, You're working.
Even when I don't feel it, You're working.
You never stop; You never stop working.
(Sinach, "Waymaker," 2015)

My faith was strengthened by the reminder that even if things didn't turn out the way we wanted or the way we expected, God was working. He was sovereign over every situation. He had a plan for us to get through this most recent fever. When the song ended, I told the guys what was happening and that I had to leave to take care of August. These men prayed for my son and for our family, and I realized that God had put these guys in my life for times such as these. I was so grateful for it. I hope each of us has a group of close friends that we can pour our hearts out to, who will genuinely care for us and always be there for us in our greatest times of need.

Parent Struggles

Blessed be the God and Father of our Lord Jesus Christ,
the Father of mercies and God of all comfort,
who comforts us in all our affliction,
so that we may be able to comfort those who are in any affliction,
with the comfort with which we ourselves are comforted by God.
2 Corinthians 1:3–4

As parents, we know that seeing our kids suffer through any illness, big or small, is like torture. We would do anything to take the sickness from our kids and bear the burden ourselves. The incredible thing Juli and I had to realize was that we were not the only ones to have gone through such a trial. Many have gone through much worse, and many have learned how to trust in God through it all. In the months following all of August's ordeal, we found ourselves having conversations with friends who were going through health crises with their own children. As a result of the comfort that we were blessed to receive, we were able to comfort those who came to us looking for answers. Even in the midst of our trial, I was incredibly comforted and encouraged by the perspective of another couple, Emily and Mike, going through health challenges with their daughter. Considering all that their daughter went through, and continues to go through, this couple displayed faith and hope that inspired Juli and I to trust in God's perfect plan in our seemingly never-ending saga. I hope Emily's words below, this story within a story, can provide the same perspective on the comfort of God for you as it did for us.

Social media post from 10/6/2020:
So about a month or so ago, my husband and I found out that we are expecting baby #3. We couldn't be more excited, especially because our two girls and baby #3 would be so close in age. A week later, I took my second daughter to her five month pediatric checkup, thinking it would be a quick visit. An ultrasound and MRI were done that week, and we quickly found out that she has hydrocephalus and needs brain surgery or else it could become fatal. It was a roller coaster of a week, from finding out we were having another baby to meeting with several neurosurgeons to figuring out the safest way to go into my daughter's brain and operate effectively. At this point, I didn't think things could get much worse. Well, after arriving home one day, I found a big puddle of water on our bathroom floor. When I looked up, I saw the leak and brown stain on the ceiling. I knew we really needed a new roof, but this just wasn't a good time with everything going on because of the health expenses we were incurring. I called our go-to roofer, Mike Rank, and asked if he could come patch it up when he had a chance. He explained he had several roofs to build that week but would make sure to come by and help us. The following day, I spent the entire day at Jersey Shore with my five month

old, meeting with doctors all over the hospital. I was so stressed out between being pregnant, not knowing what's going to happen with my daughter, and imagining what my bathroom looked like at that moment. As I sat in the car in the Jersey Shore parking lot sobbing, I begged God to lighten my load. Seconds later, I received a call from Mike. When I answered, he told me to pick out what color shingles I wanted because he wanted to replace our roof at no charge. I started to cry. I couldn't believe it. Talk about an answered prayer. He then explained that a fellow realtor and now friend, Pattie Romano, wanted to help pay for the roofing materials, and the manager, Jim, from Universal Supply Company wanted to donate a ton of roofing materials as well. And, on top of that, Mike's friend Shemick from Precision Power Washing heard what was going on and asked to power wash our home. I have never met Pattie, Jim, or Shemick at this point, but Mike shared our daughter's journey with them, and they all asked to be part of it and help us. What a blessing. My husband and I are so thankful for these wonderful people. Thank you for providing us with a high-quality roof and amazing power wash. Through all of this with our daughter, the last thing on our minds was taking care of our home, and we so appreciate you all taking that burden from us. Now, instead of my husband working 50+ hours a week to save money for a new roof, he's able to work normal hours and be with our daughter and me at her doctor visits, MRIs, and surgeries. We are grateful to be a part of this wonderful town, and we can't wait to pay it forward to another family. It truly is amazing how God works through others, and to witness such a blessing happen to our own family is so humbling. Thank you, Mike and Nicole Rank, Pattie, Jim, and Shemick.

Social media post from 10/9/2020:
So, after meeting with several neurosurgeons, it's safe to say that Gigi has been diagnosed with agenesis of the corpus callosum. Agenesis of the corpus callosum is a rare birth defect—affects one in 10,000 people—in which there is an absence of the corpus callosum, which normally separates the left and right brain and helps each side to interact with one another. While this is a rare condition and there is no cure, the neurosurgeon was confident that on a scale from mild to severe, Gigi is in the mid mild part of the scale, which is great! Even though Gigi won't be the best video gamer, with PT, OT, and speech therapy, Gigi can absolutely live a normal life! Things may not come as easily to her, but she has the best big sis and future little sibling, who are her biggest cheerleaders.

Gigi does have to go for a lumbar procedure, which we are in the process of scheduling. The reason being is that she still may have hydrocephalus as a separate issue, and they need to sedate her and go into her spine to test the CSF fluid [cerebrospinal fluid]. Should Gigi's fluid test positive, they will admit her and place a shunt in her brain then and there. Hopefully she will not test positive.

Thank you, everyone, for keeping Gigi in your prayers, and if you would continue to pray for her, that would be wonderful. Take a look at the photos from this AM—Gigi was able to hold her toy for the first time and move the toy from the left to right hand. What a big milestone for her!!!

Thank you, Jesus, for guiding us through these difficult decisions and this situation.

Social media post from 10/19/2020:
Gigi had a spinal procedure this morning in which the neurosurgeon inserted a needle between two lumbar bones to remove a sample of cerebrospinal fluid. This is the fluid that surrounds your brain and spinal cord to protect them from injury.

Due to the CSF fluid being high, the fluid was sent out to be tested for cancer, spina bifida, and several other birth defects. There is no concern at the moment, but they want to make sure just because of the CSF fluid being high.

Although it came back that her CSF fluid was higher than it should be, the neurosurgeon decided to hold off on placing a shunt in her brain, and we are going to try and monitor her hydrocephalus for now. We will be seeing the neurosurgeon often to monitor. Praise God for one less thing on Gigi's plate at this moment!!!

While we monitor the hydrocephalus, we are to also focus on the agenesis of the corpus callosum, which is currently causing hearing loss in the left ear, seizures, possibly an issue with eye sight and vertigo, and a big delay in milestones. We are seeing the cardiologist to check her heart, and the ophthalmologist, audiologist, and neurologist in the coming week.

Thank you, everyone, for your prayers and being a part of Gigi's journey so far. We have a long road ahead with many doctor visits and hospital trips to follow, but with everyone's support, it makes the hard days a little bit easier.

Social media post from 10/26/2020:
Normally, I use my Instagram blog for sharing the feels of motherhood and trying times, but I think it's important to mention this on all social media platforms.

Mike and I have been struggling to find peace in this entire situation with Gigi. It feels like we've been robbed of that joyous first year with our baby girl. The endless struggles and new concerns that arise weekly have taken a toll on us physically and mentally, but I've had several folks ask me, "How could this not take a toll on you spiritually? How could you be happy with God when He gave you this?" It's a valid question for those who don't read the Word as part of their daily routine. And sometimes I do end up in tears asking God, "Why is this happening?" I truly wish I had the answer, but I don't. What Mike and I do have, though, is the comfort of knowing that God is using our family, but most importantly Gigi, for something really special. I don't know what that is, but I'm 100% certain of it. I can feel in my heart that good will come out of this, and I can't wait to see how.

Today has been a very hard day mentally. I made the mistake of watching old videos of Bella at Gigi's age. Then, I started to scroll back to the earlier months when Bella was only two months old and quickly realized that Gigi is about where Bella was at two months, and Gigi is turning six months in the coming week. That was a very hard reality check. Things are starting to sink in.

So, instead of burying into a hole, I opened my Bible. Once I found peace and reassurance that God really is in control, I had a strong desire to understand why He gives us trials. While I knew the basic reasons, I just needed to know more. I found an article that brought me to tears because it spelled the reasons out perfectly and accompanied the reading material with more Bible verses, which I then opened my Bible to read.

In a moment where I felt so lost, I quickly gained that feeling of comfort, and I hope through this article, you can too with the trials you may currently be facing. [Article not included.]

Just want to say thank you again for your continued prayers, everyone. It means more than you'll ever be able to understand. Our faith and your support have kept us afloat these last few weeks. And it's something that will never be forgotten.

Social media post from 11/3/2020:
Update: Unfortunately, today's visit to the hospital didn't go as well as we had hoped. Gigi is losing her hearing in both ears. It was heartbreaking to hear that she likely can't recognize my and Mike's voices. We are meeting with a pediatric ENT who specializes in surgery on the inner ear. Please keep this sweet girl in your prayers. Thanks, everyone.

"'For I know the plans I have for you,' declares the Lord, 'plans to prosper you and not to harm you, plans to give you hope and a future'" (Jeremiah 29:11).

"Yes, my soul, find rest in God; my hope comes from Him. Truly He is my rock and my salvation; He is my fortress, I will not be shaken" (Psalm 62: 5–6).

Update: Prayers for this sweet girl, please. At audiologist now and not sure how things are looking.

Social media post from 11/5/2020:
Let's talk about our Ultimate Healer.

After another very hard hospital visit, I was told Gigi would lose 60% of her hearing in each ear and she would need hearing aids to hear us and surgery to fix the structure of her middle ear bones so that she doesn't go fully deaf. I was told she wouldn't laugh for at least several months after getting her hearing aids.

Fast forward two hours. Mike and I were sitting with Gigi and were playing with her as she swung in the swing. All of a sudden, she started LAUGHING. I mean a *real* belly laugh. I couldn't believe it.

Just a reminder that although doctors are smart and know a lot about medical issues, our ultimate healer is God. He can give and take away whatever He so chooses. Tonight, He chose to give Gigi the gift of laughter. And we couldn't be more thankful. What a beautiful sound to hear our daughter laugh for the first time, especially when we were told she wouldn't for a very long time.

P.S. At the end, I think Gigi got as overwhelmed as we did! We were all tearing up over such a joyful moment.

Social media post from 3/9/2021:
"He led you through the vast and dreadful wilderness, that thirsty and waterless land, with its venomous snakes and scorpions" (Deut. 8:15).

Maybe you've known that kind of wilderness. A wilderness of isolation where you've found yourself without a circle of intimate friends or without a church home. Or a wilderness of waiting that despite your prayers and pleas, continues to stretch out past your point of endurance. Maybe it's a wilderness of deep pain—something that's shattered life and you find yourself wandering a trail of despair and debris.

When I'm in a wilderness, the first thing I want is out. "How long, O Lord? When will You bring me through?" I ask God. "When will this end?" But that focus on getting *out* of the wilderness can lead us to miss all that God has for us *in* the wilderness.

Social media post from 3/23/2021:
God always provides, and His timing is perfect.

When we started this journey with Gigi, I had no idea where we were headed. We learned to walk by faith, not by sight. In the last eight months, God has completely changed our lives with Gigi's diagnosis. Gigi changed our hearts and taught us what true happiness is. I now know that true happiness lies in hearing our baby girl babbling when we were told she may never speak or seeing her persistence shine through as she reaches for a toy that's at a distance even though her muscle tone is extremely weak. We count our blessings every single day.

With that, Gigi has a very long journey ahead of her. Her weak muscle tone, hearing, and eyesight are several big areas of concern. Mike and I have felt it on our hearts over the last several months to look into relocating to another state for healthcare purposes. We found that Duke and UNC in Raleigh, North Carolina, can provide Gigi with phenomenal care for her specific condition. We have constantly prayed for God to open and close doors on such a big decision.

God has answered our prayers over the last few days with wide open doors, and it truly brings tears to my eyes. I am grateful for the plan He has for us. A spot for Gigi opened up at Duke and UNC for all 11 specialists after months of being on the wait list. Thank you, Jesus! Mike was recently offered a great position serving the needs of older folks, which he absolutely loves doing. And we found our dream lot which we will be building our forever home on.

We are really going to miss being close to family and friends and will miss our sweet, one-of-a-kind town. But we are excited to see what God has planned for our little girl and our family. We will continue to walk by faith and praise His wonderful name even when we cannot see what is ahead.

Our girls are very excited to become southern belles! As some from the south may say, "y'all's babies are happier than pigs in mud."

Social media post from 9/8/2021:
One year ago today, Gigi's MRI results came back, and our lives changed. If you had asked me 365 days ago, I would've said it changed for the worst.

But now, I can wholeheartedly say it changed for the best! This past year has taught us that each child thinks a different way, and no one way is the "right" way.

When the doctor called a year ago, she said, "I'm sorry to have to tell you this, but Gigi has been diagnosed with . . . (list all diagnoses)." I was sitting at my kitchen table in New Jersey and just wished so badly Mike was home for the call. I got off the phone with the doctor and immediately asked God for the strength to call Mike and somehow tell him everything was going to be okay when I didn't believe that myself. Luckily, God was already working on his heart because as we cried on the phone together, we became so much stronger within seconds. God provided us instant strength from that moment on to ensure the countless hospital visits, early mornings filled with fasting and blood work, late-night calls to the on-call doctors, and busy days traveling to specialists.

God provided so much more than just strength though. He provided us an amazing support system, financial help, and a clear-cut path every step of the way this past year. He quieted our minds so that the Holy Spirit was loud in our hearts.

This has been the hardest year of our lives and, I'm sure, our family's lives as they've had to watch Gigi go through a lot (*insert the waterworks*), but we are so unbelievably hopeful about our second year of this journey with Gigi because God always provides, and we have learned to trust Him wholeheartedly during the highs and lows.

We want to thank every single person who has been there for us this past year. It truly does take a village to raise a child, and we never could have gotten through this year without every single one of you. Cheers to this next year with baby Gigi. Keep proving the doctors wrong, baby girl. You've got the Ultimate Healer on your side! Thank you, Jesus, for changing our lives!

"And we know that for those who love God all things work together for good, for those who are called according to his purpose" (Romans 8:28).

Fifth Surgery (July 24, 2020)
Vesicostomy & Ureter Stent Removal

Rejoice in hope. Be patient in tribulation. Be constant in prayer.
Romans 12:12

Social Media Post

An update on August:

August was admitted to the children's hospital this past Tuesday with a fever from a UTI. The good news is that his kidneys are draining well and look so much better than before. However, we found out that his bladder is not fully emptying when he pees. Antibiotics were given for the infection, fevers are gone, and tests were done this morning to determine the issue. Based on the results, the plan is to do a vesicostomy, with a reversal at some point around 18 months. (A vesicostomy is an operation that makes an opening from the bladder to the abdomen just below the belly button. The opening lets urine drain out of the bladder.) We appreciate your prayers as he goes in for this surgery in about an hour (they will also remove the stents in the ureter at the same time).

Here are some perspectives on promises, patience, and prayer (stretching for alliteration, I know):

Promises: Rejoicing in hope means resting in the assurance of a promise. It's not just wishing that something comes true, but being assured that you know something will happen. There is always uncertainty with the outcomes of surgery, and we trust in God during this time, but how grateful we can be to have the assurance of salvation, which we rejoice in: "I write these things to you who believe in the name of the Son of God, that you may know that you have eternal life" (1 John 5:13).

Patience: This has been a time of tribulation for August's physical health, and it has taught our family a lot about patience. Just when we think one problem is fixed, another one arises. We know this will continue to be a long journey, but we can see how God is teaching us patience through these difficult times.

Prayer: Continuing steadfastly in prayer has taught us dependence on God. We know these circumstances are beyond our control, but we are grateful for the wonderful care August has received, and we trust that God will work things out according to His will.

His timing, not ours.

Will keep you posted. Thanks for your prayers.

Update: The pediatric urologist said that the surgery went well. August is back in his room with Juli. Thank you all for your thoughts, prayers, and encouragement! Love you guys.

Advocate

And if anyone sins, we have an Advocate with the Father, Jesus Christ the righteous.
1 John 2:1

The radiology staff always complimented August for being a good patient. Many of them shared that they had never seen a baby behave so well during the exams. Perhaps his familiarity with the environment and the frequency of his exams made him comfortable with being poked and prodded. While most babies cried, he just laid there, soaking it all in like a tourist sightseeing. We appreciated all of the staff that performed his numerous exams, but two visits to the radiology department stand out in my mind as somewhat out of the ordinary—situations when I had to advocate for August. These visits were for a test that I had never heard of. The deeper we got into August's care, the more I realized that pediatric health care was an entirely different world from the adult cardiopulmonary medical-surgical world I knew.

August had three voiding cystourethrograms completed during his first year of life. A VCUG is a test in which images are taken while a contrast fills and empties from the bladder. The images track the movement of urine through the urinary system. In a healthy person, urine will flow in one direction from the kidneys, through the ureters, into the bladder, and out of the body through the urethra. Once the bladder reaches a certain point of fullness, the sensation should trigger the urine to flow in this direction. However, in the case of our son, the manipulating, disconnecting, and reattaching of his ureters on both sides made the proper flow of urine challenging. The urologist told us that he has seen about two-thirds of his patients with the complexity of August's issues need additional corrective surgery after turning two years old. The problem is that urine follows the path of least resistance. If there is too much resistance for the urine to leave the body, the urine will flow back up the ureters toward the kidneys, contributing to worsening hydronephrosis and an increased risk of UTIs. Augie's first VCUG, two weeks after he was born, showed no reflux of urine up the ureters. However, his second VCUG revealed bilateral reflux, which appeared worse on the left side. One of the contributing factors was the delay of his surgery due to the COVID-19 pandemic, resulting in a thickened bladder wall as his body worked harder and harder to push urine out around the ureterocele that he was born with.

My point in sharing the details surrounding the two visits is to express the importance of what too many people have discovered when dealing with sick family members. Despite the excellent care that our son received, we experienced a number of occasions when we needed to speak up for our little guy, at a time when he couldn't speak for himself—to advocate for him.

The first opportunity (yes, I will refer to it as an opportunity) was during August's second VCUG. The time in the procedure came when August needed a urinary catheter inserted. I had mentioned to the pediatric residents that even the team at the children's hospital in New Brunswick had a difficult time inserting the catheter due to some unexpected resistance. The team of residents respectfully acknowledged my concerns as they continued on with the insertion attempt. After an unsuccessful attempt that lasted much longer and caused more pain and crying for Augie than I care to remember, the team got all new equipment and prepared for another insertion. They decided to wait a short period of time to allow August to recover from his intense bout of hysterical crying.

As the team re-entered the room for their second attempt, I requested, with all due respect, that they stop and get in touch with a pediatric nurse—in an effort to protect my son from further pain and discomfort. I knew that getting a pediatric nurse who had inserted hundreds of catheters would be a much better situation than a team of pediatric residents who collectively might have inserted 10 catheters total between the four of them up to this point in their early careers. The radiology staff got in touch with one of my coworkers who worked as a nurse in the pediatric emergency department. I knew we were in good hands as soon as she entered the room. Sure enough, she was able to insert the catheter with a few techniques that she had learned during her extensive nursing career. What would have happened if I had stood by quietly and said nothing?

Another opportunity to advocate for my son was prior to his third VCUG. At the end of my workday on the Friday before his scheduled exam, I went to the radiology department, and I was able to speak with the radiologist who would oversee August's exam. I informed him of the trouble they had with the catheter insertion. I also told him that August now had a vesicostomy. I was not sure what other precautions had to be taken for a successful VCUG now that August had another hole in his bladder. I asked this doctor to talk with all of the team members that would perform the test on the following Monday, and he assured me that the message would be passed along.

The day of the exam came, and August and I showed up in the radiology department early for the pre-VCUG ultrasound. All went smoothly with the ultrasound, and we headed back for the test. As they were setting up, I reminded them about August's vesicostomy, just in case they didn't see the giant "pee-hole" just below his belly button. I was told that everyone was aware, and they reassured me that they would still be able to perform the exam and obtain accurate diagnostic findings. When the pediatric residents arrived, they set up their supplies for the catheter insertion, and I spoke up one more time. I kindly asked them if they could simply double-check to make sure that this test could be done for a patient with a vesicostomy. They left the room and came back after about 10 minutes. I was shocked to hear them say that they were not trained or qualified to perform a VCUG on a patient with a vesicostomy and that I would have to reschedule the test at another facility. If I hadn't been in complete and utter disbelief, I probably would have responded with the anger and frustration that was boiling up inside of me. I had attempted to keep open lines of communication with every single person on that team that day and even on the days leading up to the exam. I could not believe that they were literally inches away from starting the procedure, with catheter in hand, for something that would have caused significant pain for my son and been a complete waste of time.

Outside of these two opportunities, we also had the wonderful experience of having Augie's pediatrician, Dr. Perril, intervene as his advocate. During one of August's UTIs, his fevers came on insidiously. When tasked with obtaining a clean-catch urine specimen, Juli and I made our best attempts and believed we caught what was a sufficient sample. We brought the specimen to the lab and waited to hear the results. His urologist ordered another antibiotic for treatment, and we addressed his fevers by alternating between acetaminophen and ibuprofen. The fevers were not subsiding, so I went to obtain the preliminary urine culture results from the lab. We sent the lab results to the urologist and to Augie's pediatrician on the same day. We realized that, at this point, Dr. Barone, the urologist, had seen the most complex cases when it came to urinary disorders. Due to his vast experience, he had seen cultures like this many times before. He told us to monitor his fevers and see how August felt in the morning. When Dr. Perril saw the preliminary report, she called Dr. Barone and told him that this was the worst culture she had ever seen and that Augie had to go to the hospital immediately for intense intravenous antibiotic therapy. She would not let the urologist go until she had convinced him to contact us and send us to the hospital for another admission. While we had, and still have, full confidence in Dr. Barone, Dr. Perril advocated for August in this instance so he could receive the urgent care he needed in the timeliest manner possible. Praise God for advocates!

In doing my best to be my son's advocate, how could my mind not go to the greatest Advocate of all, my Lord and Savior Jesus Christ? In 1 John 2:1, we read that, "If anyone sins, we have an Advocate with the Father, Jesus Christ the righteous." That term advocate is a legal term meaning an "intercessor" or "one who pleads another's cause." Just as August was unable to defend or speak up for himself, we, in our sin, are completely incapable of speaking up or defending ourselves before a holy and just God. Our sin has put us in a place where we stand guilty before a sovereign Judge. That verse says, "If anyone sins." We know from elsewhere in Scripture (and if we are truly honest with ourselves) that "all have sinned and fall short of the glory of God" (Romans 3:23). In a much greater sense, Jesus was not interceding so we could simply avoid an unnecessary and uncomfortable surgery but so we, as rebels, could avoid the lost eternity that we fully deserve. He entered the scene to plead a case for helpless sinners who could in no way defend ourselves. Jesus is described as the righteous One. He is the only one who is worthy enough to approach God the Father on our behalf as He took our sin upon Himself and bore the judgment that we deserved so we might be granted the forgiveness of sins and receive His righteousness (Acts 4:12; 2 Corinthians 5:21).

When it comes to *being* an advocate, I hope that you will speak up with boldness, out of love for your friend or family member who may need you. When it comes to *having* an advocate, I pray that you can say with conviction that you know you need one and declare with confidence that you have one in the Lord Jesus Christ. "For when we were still without strength, in due time Christ died for the ungodly" (Romans 5:6). What joy!

No Longer a Nurse, Not Yet IT

To everything there is a season, a time for every purpose under heaven.
Ecclesiastes 3:1

As if this year was not out-of-control enough already, I figured the best thing to do would be to attempt to make a major career change mid-pandemic. I had actually applied for a new position in the early months of 2020, prior to the arrival of the first cases of COVID-19 in our region. Applying for the position was a very difficult decision for me since I had spent the last eight years of my nursing career in the clinical education department at Monmouth Medical Center. While I was working as a nurse educator, my department had always turned to me whenever it needed IT support. I had an interest in clinical informatics, so when the opportunity came up to work in that field with my current employer, I decided to apply. I sat with the person who was leaving that position to get a feel for the position. I appreciated the time she gave me, but I still had only a foggy idea of what to expect.

When my employer offered me the job, I faced the very difficult decision of whether to accept the offer or not. It had been tough to even apply for this position because I loved my current job, my coworkers, and my boss. I wanted to ensure that this would be the right decision—not just the best move for my career but also for my personal life and my family. After much prayer, conversations with loved ones, and some back-and-forth with corporate HR, I accepted the position as the regional informatics site manager at MMC and MMC Southern Campus.

If my move into nursing education had been one step away from being a "real" nurse, moving into clinical informatics was another huge step away. In my educator role, I still had occasional opportunities for bedside patient care and my clinical skills were kept up-to-date while providing rapid response team coverage. Clinical informatics would pull me even further from the bedside. After spending a few weeks as just one of two clinical people in the IT department, I quickly learned how little I knew. I had been the go-to-guy in nursing education. Now, I felt as if I were living in a foreign land with no knowledge of the native language. Despite getting more comfortable with the responsibilities in my new role, I still had a tough time telling people what I actually did for work. When asked, I found the best way to answer that question was to explain that my job was to take people's problems and give them to other people. The best description I have found is that I support the healthcare team with the management of the clinical information documentation system.

I accepted the job in April 2020, but due to the emergent need to cross-train staff for COVID-19 patient care, I did not transfer until August 2020.

Books & Birthdays

All Scripture is given by inspiration of God, and is profitable for doctrine, for reproof, for correction, for instruction in righteousness, that the man of God may be complete, thoroughly equipped for every good work.
2 Timothy 3:16

Drive-by birthday celebrations were a trend that came and went in 2020. Everybody was doing it, they seemed cute and exciting, but they were kind of uncomfortable. We actually did appreciate that we could bring a smile to a child's face just by driving by and beeping our car horn while holding a birthday sign out the window. Maggie was old enough to know that her duty as a 6-year-old was to beg us for a drive-by birthday party. This socially distant alternative to a birthday party would have been nice, but my daughter deserved more. Our family decided to make a trip out to south-central Pennsylvania. You might be thinking, "How in the world is south-central Pennsylvania more exciting than a drive-by birthday party?" But we were going to spend a family weekend at the camp that our kids have grown to love, even at a young age.

Greenwood Hills Camp and Conference Center is the camp that multiple generations of my family had attended. In addition to the kids' camps and family camps, my grandfather had a private home built on the campground many years ago, so we planned to have Maggie's birthday celebration there. The camp is down the road from Caledonia State Park. This beautiful natural habitat has trails, lakes, and mountains, so we decided to drive through the park and go on a fun, uphill hike to the top of one of the small mountains. The other exciting part of this trip was that Maggie hiked with her cousins. My sister and her kids live in Lancaster, so we typically see them a few times each year. But, due to all of the happenings of 2020, we had not seen them for quite some time.

Our hike was a challenging uphill walk with a small, yet steep, rock climb at the end. While Juli and the younger kids chose to walk around it (Augie in a baby carrier), Maggie and a few of her cousins traversed the vertical terrain. On the top of the mountain, we had a breathtaking view of the treetops. We took a few photos, and we gave Maggie a present that she was thrilled to receive: the next book in Andrew Peterson's *Wingfeather* series.

The pandemic had given us plenty of time to read as we spent countless hours at home. We started off the early months of the COVID-19 pandemic by revisiting one of my favorite series, which I read as a child: C. S. Lewis's *The Chronicles of Narnia*. I have a terrible memory, so I felt as if I were reading parts of these books for the very first time. This was my first experience seeing my kids get excited about reading. Granted, they were bigger fans of being read *to* than reading themselves, but they would ask me to read more of each book as we worked through this series. As most people are aware, Lewis filled this series with allegory and symbolism related to his Christian faith. Our reading through this series led to many conversations about eternal things as our kids asked deeper and deeper questions up until the final book.

When we completed the *Narnia* books, we began to read the *Wingfeather* series. Personally, I think I was a bigger fan of these books than my kids were, but it was exciting to see my children beg me to keep reading. They seemed to want the story to never end. These books are jam-packed with insight on how to deal with interpersonal conflict, especially among siblings—very appropriate for four young kids who seemed to be at war with each other, especially when confined to tight living quarters for an extended period of time. The books also teach reliance on the Maker when the main characters' constant adventures seem too much for them to bear.

Sometimes, I would read ahead as my kids fell asleep because I was intrigued by what I would find next. I really enjoyed the writing style, and it actually led me into a little bit of an Andrew Peterson kick. I was first introduced to him when my sister-in-law showed me his song *Is He Worthy?* I did not realize that this Christian singer-songwriter was also an author. In the middle of the *Wingfeather* series, I picked up another one of the author's books called *Adorning the Dark*. It actually inspired me to record this account of all the events that transpired surrounding our son.

These books helped us journey through the pandemic, but we really did rely on one Book to carry us through the real-life adventures of 2020. Feeling trapped at home but escaping to another imaginary world was exciting. We had an opportunity to talk about how great it can feel when reading takes us to another place, but we also wanted to remind our kids of keeping first things first. While these books were entertaining, my wife and I shared the impact of the most life-changing book we have ever read. "The Word of God is living and powerful, and sharper than any two-edged sword, piercing even to the division of soul and spirit, and of joints and marrow, and is a discerner of the thoughts and intents of the heart" (Hebrews 4:12). Books have the ability to make us think, but no other book has the ability to eternally transform an individual's life than the Word of God, the Bible. The many verses of Scripture that I have shared throughout these memories really strengthened our faith and provided the hope that we needed to press on. We knew that the Word had prepared us for these troublesome days, and we knew that we were growing through the process of trusting God through it all.

Daily Care & Maintenance

Come to Me all you who are weary and heavily burdened and I will give you rest.
Matthew 11:28

Throughout August's journey, he would often come home with different needs and various tubes and bags. He was by far our neediest child, but we did not develop any sort of resentment or hesitancy to do what it would take to support him. The antibiotics were nonstop as August was on either a prophylactic dose once or twice per day or a more frequent treatment dose for his recurrent UTIs. For a brief time, we were tasked with managing bilateral nephrostomy tubes at home too. Ensuring these drainage bags stayed below the level of his bladder and were emptied frequently enough to prevent overfilling was not too difficult, but when you consider the movement of a baby, the biggest challenge was keeping August from tugging at the tubes or getting tangled up in them. August had an indwelling urinary catheter on a number of occasions, and we impressed ourselves by finding the perfect "hooks" for hanging his drainage bag below the level of his bladder but above the floor: from dresser handles, rocking chair legs, and crib frames to stroller legs and high chair steps. We found the biggest challenge was carrying him around the house with all these additional lines and tubes.

One of the more challenging daily tasks was changing August's diapers during the four months following his vesicostomy. I had changed diapers on adults for almost five years of my nursing career and more than six years in my parenting career. So, with a total time span of 11 years developing my diaper-changing skills, you would think that I could have handled anything. The challenge I faced was that I had never been tasked with caring for a patient or a child with two "pee-holes" (the technical healthcare term). In addition to August peeing out of his urethra like a normal boy, he had an additional hole below his belly button (which the vesicostomy created). This allowed urine to constantly seep out of his bladder. We tried shifting his diaper to be higher in the front. We attempted purchasing oversized diapers that would go well up his back and much higher than his belly button. We placed layers of gauze inside the diaper over the vesicostomy site to soak up the urine. Unfortunately, August's movements during both day and night prevented any of these plans from working. We found that the best way to keep August dry and maintain his skin integrity (especially during the night) was to lay an open diaper across the lower portion of his abdomen and tuck it inside of his traditionally worn diaper. We had a 65 percent success rate with this method as the "belly" diaper would often slip out from underneath the other diaper and August would soak his pajamas, sheets, and entire crib. It felt as if we were changing his sheets almost every night.

When Augie had his vesicostomy, the medical team informed us that this new anatomical setup could last as long as a year and a half. In addition to the challenges of keeping August dry and keeping his vesicostomy free of infection, we were spending twice as much on diapers since he needed two almost all the time. More than the financial strain, the daily burden of managing this complex anatomy was draining (no pun intended). Juli and I prayed for wisdom and strength and endurance, knowing that this setup was necessary for the time being. But we took comfort in knowing that this season would end. How ecstatic we were when we found out that August's vesicostomy would be reversed much sooner than expected.

Dexter

For the wrath of man does not produce the righteousness of God.
James 1:20

We figured our lives were still too boring up to this point and Dexter wanted to get in on the action. Perhaps it was an extreme reaction due to a severe lack of attention, but Dexter did not want his younger brother to be the only one who got to enjoy fun-filled trips to the hospital. On a cold and silent night in October, he was joyfully playing with a new toy, bouncing around the hallways and having the time of his life. Sure enough, Dexter eventually slipped and fell. The entire toy was made of a soft material, but on the handle was a small plastic zip tie. The sharp point on the end of this tiny securement device cut deeply along the outside of his left nostril. The bleeding was enough that we decided to go to the emergency department at my hospital to be safe. Dexter handled it like a champ. They determined that he did not need stitches but simply a good cleaning and some industrial-strength skin adhesive to aid the healing and minimize the scarring.

On an equally cold and silent night in October, exactly one week later, Dexter decided to start climbing our bookshelf. Now, as I begin this story, one might assume that he climbed too high, fell down, and ended up needing to go to the hospital. However, to my shame, I was the one who led to our visit to the emergency room. As Dexter continued to climb, I yelled at him to get down. He scurried down, and I chased him to his room for his time out. In my fury, as I yelled at him about the dangers of climbing bookshelves, the inevitable happened. He tripped on the ladder of his bunk bed and fell headfirst toward the floor. Before he could hit the floor, the corner of a wooden drawer that had been left open decided to get in the way. He immediately started to scream. I flipped him over, and the blood was everywhere. In the middle of his forehead was a gash so deep I could not see the bottom of it. I took a shirt and applied pressure to it as best I could while carrying him to the kitchen.

One week prior, we had discussed at length whether Dexter needed to be brought to the hospital for the gash by his nostril. But this was clearly a situation that needed medical attention. Once we slowed the bleeding, we hopped in the car and raced to the hospital. After receiving a few greetings of "welcome back," we quickly made it to the pediatric emergency room. Some of the staff had recognized me as a coworker, but unfortunately, due to the year we were having, I was more familiar to the staff as the father of their patients. I had gotten all too familiar with being on the other end of the needle. I was learning to appreciate the services that my employer now offered to me and my family as patients.

While we waited, the staff cleaned the wound and contacted the on-call plastic surgeon. It just so happened that I had worked with this surgeon before and I had his cell number saved in my phone. Unfortunately, he had been called to another hospital for an emergency, and he would not be available for multiple hours. The staff decided to temporarily secure and close up Dexter's wound with some steri-strips and have us come back early tomorrow morning. They assured us that if we kept the wound clean and returned for stitches in the morning, everything would be fine. We went home planning to return the next morning.

When it came time to stitch up his wound, the staff removed the steri-strips, and we could finally see how deep the cut was. After injecting the area with a numbing agent, the plastic surgeon had to stitch the wound in two layers: one deep and another at the surface. Once again, the staff told Dexter he was the bravest boy for doing so well. I am pretty certain the staff tell that to every kid, but Dexter barely even cried the entire time. We were incredibly grateful that this surgeon coordinated everything and made this a quick treat-and-release hospital visit. It was pretty neat to see Dexter ask for extra stickers for his brothers and sister. Upon our arrival at home, Maggie, Wesley, and August received their sticker gifts, and soon, we were bombarded with requests for more trips to the hospital. No thank you.

I think I learned my lesson that weekend. If I had calmly spoken to my son as he was putting himself in harm's way, we could have avoided this situation. My anger caused me to yell and chase him back to his room, ultimately resulting in his injury. I was reminded of James 1:20, which states, "For the wrath of man does not produce the righteousness of God." I thought I could drive the disobedience out of my child's heart and bring him to a point of doing what's right. However, the Word of God tells us to be "swift to hear, slow to speak, and slow to wrath" (James 1:19). My wrath just led to more headaches, literally and figuratively. We had spent enough time in hospitals this year already, and I had no intention of adding any more trips.

Loved Ones

Many of us lost loved ones during 2020—whether to COVID-19 or otherwise. Either way, the losses were devastating, especially when we did not get a chance to say our goodbyes. Juli's grandmother passed during this time, and although she had ongoing health issues, the pandemic did not make things any easier. Our plans to visit her in the summer of 2020 were sidelined due to the pandemic, and we did not have a chance to get out there for her to meet her newest great-grandchildren. May we use the disruption of the pandemic as a wake-up call and reminder to cherish and appreciate the family and friends who had the deepest impact on our lives. I will share a post about one example of an individual with a tremendous impact on me whom we lost in 2020:

Social Media Post (November 4, 2020)

The highlight of so many years in the past decade of my life was attending the men's Bible studies with Randy Amos. Whether at Camp Horizon, Pine Bush, or Greenwood Hills, I looked forward to these not simply for the great fellowship but also for the opportunity to sit under the sound of this man's teaching. I have never met someone with the ability to humbly yet confidently make the complex things of Scripture so clear to my mind. He was such a godly example to me, always reminding me of the joy in knowing the Lord Jesus Christ as my Savior and helping me to rest in the promises found in the Word. Praying for Sylvia [Randy's wife] and the rest of the family.

Sixth Surgery (November 23, 2020)

With each new trip to New Brunswick, we never knew when our final visit would come. The drive up Route 18 became all too familiar—the GPS very quickly became a thing of the past. The journey up the highway and into the Plum Street Parking Garage in the city seemed shorter and shorter each time we did it. It became a bonding time for August and me as we prepared for the next step in his healing. I often prayed for his protection and success in whatever interventions were about to take place. Due to the distance, I would typically leave the car in the parking garage for the entire length of the hospital stay while my wife stayed home to care for the other kids. I had quickly learned that August loved, missed, and preferred his mommy to me. The urgency of this most recent trip prior to August's sixth major surgery found me in a familiar place since Juli preferred that I get August settled into his room after navigating through the emergency department. We had switched places before, and the easiest way for this to happen was for Juli to load up the other three kids, drive up to the children's hospital, and trade places. I would give Juli the other car keys—so she could get the car from the parking garage and drive August home upon discharge—and I would drive the minivan home.

This had been our routine, but when we realized that August would be staying at the hospital for an extended stay, I asked my dad to drive me up to get my car. Rather than leave it in the parking garage, I figured it would be best to bring it home and then drive back up to the hospital to pick up Juli and August when they were ready to come home. When we arrived, I walked up to find my car. I unlocked it and hopped in the driver seat. No one could ever accuse me of keeping a clean and spotless car, but something looked off. The mess that I typically leave in my front seat appeared a little messier. The floor on the passenger side, which was typically clear, had a clutter of papers all over it. As I looked back at the passenger side rear door, I noticed the quarter glass was broken. I realized that my car had been broken into. This was the straw that broke the camel's back. I asked myself if things could get any worse as I sat there on the verge of tears. I quickly looked through the car to see what was stolen. As I went through the trunk and the back seat, I was surprised to find that it looked like nothing had been stolen. I even had my brother's expensive power tools in the trunk, and they were still there despite evidence of someone rummaging through it. I considered filing a police report, but after calling the parking garage attendants and speaking with a few police officer friends, I realized that it may not be worth all the trouble. I also reached out to my car guy, who told me that the cost to replace that broken quarter window was not that bad.

I decided to hop in the car and head home. While speaking with my wife on the phone and sharing that nothing was stolen, I slowly realized that I had left a backpack in the back seat. I looked back again to check, and it was indeed missing. I was quite disappointed; it was my favorite backpack. But I was grateful to know that I had only lost about 10 T-shirts, six pairs of underwear and socks, some shorts and pants, and a pair of electric hair clippers. Perhaps the realization of how little had been stolen made the situation more bearable. Perhaps the fact that the thief broke the smallest and least expensive window to repair made it more tolerable. Perhaps the rationalization that the person who stole it might have needed some extra clothes and would benefit from his new wardrobe helped to alleviate my frustrations. I think the greatest peace that came from this situation was the realization that compared to all that August was about to endure, this trial seemed light. The events of Augie's hospital stay are summarized in the posts below.

Social Media Post (November 23, 2020)

Prayers appreciated for August . . .

August was admitted 11 days ago for recurrent UTIs and is scheduled tomorrow morning for a left lower ureter "detour" (connecting his lower ureter to the upper one for better drainage) to eliminate the urinary reflux and a right upper pole heminephrectomy (removal of upper portion of right kidney, which never functioned). We appreciate prayers for our little fighter.

During the uncertainties of this entire year and the unexpected challenges that many people have faced, I was recently reminded of the reality of the Hebrews 13:8: "Jesus Christ is the same yesterday, today, and forever." We slowly learned that August's condition would bring us on a long journey requiring multiple surgeries, but this particular visit was not a scheduled one. Despite the unpredictability of life, we have experienced the reality of God's faithfulness and the stability of putting our faith and trust in Jesus Christ. Every day is a new adventure, but the solid foundation that our faith is resting on has carried us through the unknown.

We truly value your prayers, and we know that God, in His sovereignty, has brought August to exactly where he needs to be.

Update: Good news . . . After a short 12 hours, August is finally out of surgery and in recovery. He is doing well, and the pediatric urologist and robotic surgeon were happy with the end result. Longer than expected due to some "hiccups" along the way, but all is well. They also reversed his vesicostomy, which was not originally planned. Thank you so much for your thoughts and prayers. Please pray that he is able to pee tomorrow when they remove the catheter. Love you all!

Social Media Post (November 26, 2020)

Thankful for so many things: For friends who made us the incredible turkey (and our church family and neighbors who have provided meals for us), for my kids who teach me how immature I am/how much I need to grow up, and for my wife. New respect for all that she does at home when I'm at work and for the exhausting work of caring for August after surgery. After a successful surgery and some progress, he is still unable to fully empty his bladder on his own, so he and Juli are still at the hospital. Thank you all for your continued prayers.

But, on this Thanksgiving 2020, looking back on what our family has gone through, would I ask to go through it again? No. But am I thankful for what I have learned of God's faithfulness and my need to leave it all in His hands?

Absolutely.

It's easy to be thankful for the "good" things, but whatever your beliefs or background may be, the words of Scripture in Romans 5:3–4 have proven so true: "And not only that, but we also rejoice in tribulations, knowing that tribulation produces perseverance; and perseverance, character; and character, hope."

One song has encouraged me through these last few months, and despite the music video making me feel like I'm back in the 90s, the message speaks volumes to me today:

Faithful from the beginning
You felt my pain, You have been where I've been
I hear You say, "It is finished."
It is written, we win in the end.

Heart's under fire, I'm facing defeat
So close to surrender, to my enemies
But Love came from heaven, to fight for me
When I am defenseless, You climb in the trenches
When I am defenseless, You climb in the trenches
The trenches with me
 (Chuck Butler, Ethan Hulse, and Tauren Wells, "Trenches," 2020)

Romans 5:5–6 goes on to say, "Now hope does not disappoint, because the love of God has been poured out in our hearts by the Holy Spirit who was given to us. For when we were still without strength, in due time Christ died for the ungodly."

Last but not least, I am thankful for my Lord and Savior Jesus Christ, who has promised to give and has certainly provided an abundant life (John 10:10).

So many things to be thankful for. I hope that everyone had a wonderful Thanksgiving.

Social Media Post from Juli (November 28, 2020)

Nine months ago, this beautiful boy and I were in the same setting, although the circumstances were a bit different. At that time, it was the joy of bringing a brand-new baby into the world, and today, it is the joy of seeing my baby smile again after an intense surgery. It has been a crazy nine months, but I can say that I feel the same joy. This joy doesn't flow naturally.

In the book of Nehemiah, we read about the Israelites rebuilding the wall around Jerusalem that was destroyed while they were in exile. Despite being surrounded by enemies, the wall was successfully built because God was with His people. Afterward, they celebrated and listened to the Word of God read to them but began to be sad because of their own sin and failures to uphold the law. In chapter eight, verse 10, Nehemiah says to the people, "This is a sacred day before our Lord. Don't be dejected and sad, for the joy of the LORD is your strength!" So they went on, in verse 12, "to celebrate with great joy because they had heard God's words and understood them." Joy in the Lord comes from being in His Word and understanding it.

We still have a journey ahead of us with August's care and recovery, but we rest in God's Word, that the joy of the Lord is our strength!

Donations

Following August's extensive surgery, in which his vesicostomy was reversed and his ureters were repaired, the urologist noted that August was not completely emptying his bladder. In the hospital, he had to have a urinary catheter reinserted. I could not believe that we were still having issues after this major surgery, when we had been told it should resolve his problems. The urologist reassured us that this would often occur following vesicostomy reversals as Augie's body had to relearn how to respond to the stimuli of his bladder filling up and forcing the urine down the urethra. We were relieved to know that the vesicostomy was gone (after initially being told he might need to have it for 18 more months), but we were trying to grapple with the reality of being told that we might need to straight catheterize our son every four hours over the course of a year. The medical supply company had already arranged for all of the supplies to be delivered in anticipation of this process.

In order to allow time for August to heal, he went home with an indwelling catheter, and we were instructed to leave it in place for two weeks. Following the two weeks, I was to remove the catheter, and we were to begin performing straight catheters. Historically, people had a difficult time inserting August's catheters due to his complex anatomy and extensive surgical history. I was very comfortable with inserting catheters into adults, but I was concerned since I had no experience with catheterizing children.

When we first attempted August's intermittent catheterizations, it was quite an adventure. Juli tried to keep him still as I worked at maintaining my sterile field. I attempted the insertion, but I was met with the same resistance that so many others had experienced before me. Not wanting to force the issue and cause other complications, we decided to wait another hour or so before trying again. Thankfully, August peed on his own without a catheter in that next hour. We were cautiously optimistic as we were told to weigh his diapers to ensure that he was emptying his bladder. His urologist said that he has seen families needing to catheterize their kids for up to two years following the type of procedures that August had. As August continued to pee on his own, we kept a careful log of his urine output and reported them back to the urologist. To say we were thrilled would be an understatement when we heard that August would not need to be catheterized at all if he continued to empty his bladder as well as he did. Time after time and surgery after surgery we had heard the all-familiar story of "Everything went well *but* . . ." We were exhausted at this point, and there was no better news to hear than August not needing any more surgeries at that time. In fact, after a number of follow-up appointments and ultrasounds, we learned that he would not need the corrective surgery that often occurred months down the road since the last surgery had fixed his reflux issue.

So, what were we supposed to do with all of these medical supplies that our insurance had already paid for? We had boxes of catheter insertion kits and intermittent urinary catheters that were (thankfully for us) completely useless at this point. For obvious reasons, the company told us that they could not take any products back once they were delivered. So we started to think of how these expensive supplies could accomplish more than just collecting dust in our garage. We had about 600 kits and 500 catheters whose estimated value was around $5,000. Thankfully, a missionary organization that our church works closely with got our supplies up to Canada to be shipped out to several medical mission stations in Zambia. We were so pleased to find out that these supplies would not go to waste.

Seventh Surgery (January 15, 2021)

Social Media Post

Round 7 (I think): August is going back now for the removal of a ureteral stent that was left in during the last surgery to aid proper healing. Trying to climb out of the crib, intentionally banging his head on the railings, and tearing off his hospital gown are his new favorite things. Should be a quick one. Thank you all for your prayers.

Update: This 10-minute surgery was sooo much better than August's last 12-hour surgery. All is done, had a quick recovery, and we are on our way home already. Thank you for your thoughts and prayers! Praise God.

Thank You Letter

It would not be appropriate for us to end our reflection on this wild year without sharing our gratitude for so many who came alongside us with such wonderful expressions of love. The letter below was a letter that we wrote to our little church family as they really helped carry us through. However, we know that each and every friend, family member, neighbor, and loved one that reached out during 2020 was part of the reason we were able to persevere. I want to bring us back to 1 Peter 1:6-7:

"In this you greatly rejoice, though now for a little while, if need be, you have been grieved by various trials, that the genuineness of your faith, being much more precious than gold that perishes, though it is tested by fire, may be found to praise, honor, and glory at the revelation of Jesus Christ."

These various trials that grieved us have ultimately brought us to a place of immense rejoicing. We found faith. We found hope. It was not in how capable our family was in mustering up these traits on our own. It was whom we put our faith in. It was where we found our hope. My prayer for my own family is that we will look back on these memories and remember God's faithfulness. My prayer for you and your loved ones is that you will find the same comfort and hope that was made ever so real to us in 2020.

Dear chapel family,

This thank-you letter is long overdue as we have been overwhelmed by the love, encouragement, and support that you have poured out on us since August's first surgery in May. The last nine months have been filled with more doctor's appointments, radiology tests, surgeries, and hospitalizations than we would have ever imagined or even thought possible, but the practical care and concern you have shown to us has been a true blessing. We are indeed thankful for the groceries, meals, gifts, and acts of kindness that have carried us through this challenging year. We know it's been a difficult year for everyone, which makes your expressions of love that much more appreciated. So often, friends and coworkers will ask how we can even begin to cope with all that August has gone through, and my honest response is, "We have a great God, and He has an incredible family!"

To share the most recent update, August's appointment last week was very positive, and his surgeon was very happy with how August is recovering. His surgical incisions look good, and he is peeing well. We have not needed to catheterize August at all, which we attribute to the many prayers that have been lifted on his behalf. We know that God is able to heal August and that He has placed us exactly where we need to be.

We know that no matter what happens, God is in control, and we praise Him for His sovereignty and His faithfulness. Thank you so much for living out 1 John 4:7–8 and showing us the love of God in such a real way. We love and appreciate all of you.

"Blessed be the God and Father of our Lord Jesus Christ, the Father of mercies and God of all comfort, who comforts us in all our affliction so that we may be able to comfort those who are in any affliction, with the comfort with which we ourselves are comforted by God" (2 Corinthians 1:3–4).

Trusting in Him,

Joey & Juli (with Maggie, Wesley, Dexter, and August)

INTERLUDE

As we transition from Part I and its focus on God's faithfulness to Part II and its focus on the power of the Word of God, I would like to revisit a verse that has become the theme of this season of life. In Job 1:21, Job declares, "The Lord gave, and the Lord takes away, blessed be the name of the Lord." Why would he have that response, and why would I even dare to suggest that we should respond in like manner? I suggest to you that it is because of God's goodness. Not only is God good, but He faithfully acts in accordance with His character (Psalm 119:68). The psalmist in the aforementioned verse declares that God's actions are a direct revelation of who He truly is, but He reminds us that this is something that we must learn. Throughout our lives, the process of learning comes in many forms. At times, we learn by listening or by watching others, but one of the best ways to have the most impactful learning is by experience. We see this in higher education as nursing students are subject to a clinical experience in the hospital setting, or when education majors participate in student teaching within a school setting. Learning by experience is one of the most powerful ways of learning, but it is perhaps one of the most painful, uncomfortable, and challenging ways to learn. But what I have found is that the more difficult that life becomes, the easier it is to look back and see the goodness of God. In these past few years, Juli and I can echo the words of David by stating, "Oh taste and see that the Lord is good. Blessed is the man who trusts in Him" (Psalm 34:8). We have experientially *tasted* the goodness of God. Often, we found the circumstances a bit tough to chew on or difficult to swallow, but we have found ourselves blessed as we learned to trust in Him.

God is good…in the giving…and in the taking.

To recap Part I (and my apologies as you could have saved yourself a great deal of time if I just told you to jump to this Interlude), 2020 can be summarized by the following verse: "A man plans his ways, but the Lord directs his steps" (Proverbs 16:9). That year was marked by unplanned trials, but we were not left without guidance on how to handle those trials that we endured. Many of these verses spoke volumes to us as I have previously mentioned, but I share them here once again to encourage you in the midst of your trials:

"And not only that, but we also glory in tribulations, knowing that tribulation produces perseverance; and perseverance, character; and character, hope."
–Romans 5:3-4

"For I reckon that the sufferings of this present time are not worthy to be compared with the glory that shall be revealed in us."
–Romans 8:18

"My brethren, count it all joy when you fall into various trials, knowing that the testing of your faith produces patience. But let patience have its perfect work, that you may be perfect and complete, lacking nothing. If any of you lacks wisdom, let him ask of God, who gives to all liberally and without reproach, and it will be given to him. But let him ask in faith, with no doubting, for he who doubts is like a wave of the sea driven and tossed by the wind."
–James 1:2-6

"The Lord gave" us August on February 28, 2020, and we had our hands full. I was preparing for a new job as we were preparing for a baby and the world was preparing for a pandemic. Finding out that he needed multiple surgeries and navigating through all of his care was overwhelming. One unsuccessful surgery after another proved exhausting. Through all of the ups and downs, we *loved* the outcome. A year that required us to live by faith caused us to reflect on what it means to trust in the Lord's plan. There were temptations, however, to give up hope when plans did not go our way.

What is the *opposite* of faith? Is it doubt…or fear…or anxiety? In a year that could easily be characterized by anxiety, we found ourselves leaning on 2 Timothy 2:13. Even when I was faithless (and filled with more anxiety than I could have ever imagined), He remained faithful. And, if God is faithful (in the giving *and* the taking), how can we do anything except bless and praise His name? Our constantly swaying emotions are ever dependent on our circumstances. Are we really supposed to base whether we bless His name on something so unstable? Certainly not! *We* are faithless, but *He* is faithful. *He* is trustworthy. *He* is dependable. *His* plan is perfect.

Our prayers, appeals, and anxieties were lifted up to our heavenly Father and He responded by covering us with a peace beyond measure.

"Be anxious for nothing but in everything, by prayer and supplication, let your requests be made known to God, and the peace of God which surpasses all understanding will guard your hearts and minds in Christ Jesus."
–Philippians 4:6-7

This was the hardest thing that we had ever gone through as individuals, as a couple, and as a family, but God's faithfulness was what we needed, and it is what we received. Many mornings, we were separated as husband and wife–one of us in the hospital with August; one at home with the other kids–but we were reminded of this promise:

"Because of the LORD's great love
We are not consumed,
For His compassions never fail.

They are new every morning;
Great is Your faithfulness."
–Lamentations 3:22-23

By way of introduction and to give you a preview of Part II, 2022 taught us the power of the Word of God. This year can be summed up for us in Psalm 119:92, "Unless your law had been my delight, I would have perished in my affliction." Whereas 2020 was a year that God indeed reminded us of his faithfulness, 2022 was a year that caused us to fully experience the reality of the living and powerful Word of God.

"For the word of God is living and active. Sharper than any double-edged sword, it pierces even to dividing soul and spirit, joints and marrow. It judges the thoughts and intentions of the heart."
–Hebrews 4:12

The Lord "took away" Jude on July 5, 2022, and we cannot count the innumerable tears that were shed in the early discovery of his diagnosis, the journey towards his birth and the days that followed. However, I want to ask you the following question. When we consider the things in life that have torn us apart emotionally, when was the last time that the Word of God brought you to tears? Perhaps it was at the point of salvation like the men gathered at Jerusalem in Acts 2:36-38:

"'Therefore, let all the house of Israel know assuredly that God has made this Jesus, whom you crucified, both Lord and Christ.' Now when they heard this, they were cut to the heart, and said to Peter and the rest of the apostles, 'Men and brethren, what shall we do?' Then Peter said to them, 'Repent, and let every one of you be baptized in the name of Jesus Christ for the remission of sins; and you shall receive the gift of the Holy Spirit.'"

I wouldn't say that I was not taking the Word of God seriously, but perhaps at times I was reading it too casually and the Word became *more* living and *more* powerful to me than ever before. Perhaps God had to bring me to this place where I was such an emotional wreck so He could speak to me, and I would actually listen.

I could not remember the last time that I cried myself to sleep, but after hearing of Jude's diagnosis back in March, I lay awake in bed sobbing.

But looking into the Word at that moment, God brought me to the *exact passages* that I needed, or more likely, He brought my *heart* to the *exact place* that it needed to be to allow His Word to speak to me.

I thank God for friends that would text me Bible verses daily and call to share how the Lord was speaking to them. One friend shared how much the Lord was carrying him through his personal struggles as he read through the book of Psalms. Seeing the power of the Word of God in his life through this portion of Scripture led me to do the same for the months leading up to Jude's birth.

King David most likely wrote almost half of the 150 psalms we find in the Bible and many of these psalms have been categorized in various ways–Psalms of praise, thanksgiving, salvation, lament, etc.

I often mistakenly think of these psalms as songs written by David in a modern fashion: as isolated attempts at recording a #1 single to top the music charts. However, similar to many honest songwriters today, David wrote these songs as he was led by the Spirit and poured out his heart in anguish, in praise, in desperation during some of the most intense moments of his life. Only a few of David's psalms give the background (e.g., Psalm 3 when he fled for his life from his son, Absalom; Psalm 51 when Nathan confronted him regarding his sin with Bathsheba; Psalm 57 as he was fleeing from Saul). But we realize that each of these songs was an outpouring of his heart in the midst of trials, tragedy, and celebration.

The psalms of lament stood out to me and spoke to me in the moments I needed them the most. In some of these psalms (Psalms 13, 55, and 71), we see David's *felt* reality versus his *actual* reality. I encourage you to read these and see for yourself. There exists an objective reality vs. a subjective perception. In today's society, the postmodern thought of standpoint theory suggests that an individual's personal experience and perspective are the ultimate source of authority and truth.

If this were the case for David, then God had abandoned him as he wrote Psalm 13. That's how he felt so that *must* be the reality, right? Of course not! How helpful it was for me to see David pouring out his heart to God but then realizing the objective truth of who God was partway through many of his psalms. His personal testimony was that God is always good.

But how did David feel as he ran for his life or when he faced life-altering uncertainties? Perhaps like Job felt in Job 13:15, "Though He slay me, yet I will trust in Him." Or Psalm 51:8, "Let the bones You have broken rejoice."

Through the pain and sorrow expressed in these psalms of lament, we learned of God's sovereignty, His wisdom, His faithfulness and love.

This is what carried us through our situation with Jude. We were praying for a miracle, but as a friend reminded me, perhaps it was by the grace of God that we knew of his diagnosis ahead of time. Although these months were extremely hard, we never appreciated or cherished any other pregnancy quite so much. And God used that time to prepare our hearts to accept His will, whatever that would be.

Now that you know the ending of our story, perhaps you might want to skip over the rest of this book. But it's not always about the ending, right? It's often about the journey we take to get there. If you are in need of encouragement or hope, I pray that you will take the time to read the pages that follow and that you will find what we found: that the Word of God has the power to carry you through your sorrow and that complete dependence on God is an incredibly good place to find yourself in.

INTRODUCTION II

I really wish this second part of our family's story did not have to be written. Yes, partly due to the fact that I am lazy and exhausted from writing, but also because I *really* like how the first part ended. I was excited to share that portion of our lives because it finished with a happy ending. We were hoping for smooth sailing moving forward with a happy and healthy little August. In fact, when I finished compiling all of the previous thoughts, life was going pretty well for us. However, it would not be fair for me to ignore these next chapters in our lives for a number of reasons: Not fair because I would be painting a picture that did not tell the whole story. Not fair because a half-painted canvas only reveals a fraction of reality. Life is filled with success stories and happy endings, but it is often equally filled with failures, disappointments, sorrow, and heartbreak.

And so, begins the story of Jude. Despite the tragedy that unfolded, we were able to get a glimpse of the completed work of art as God painted the rest of the stunning masterpiece for us, revealing a beauty we could not have anticipated.

While most of what was written about August was retrospective, the story of Jude will be built upon the foundation of journal entries and reflections that we recorded as the events transpired. My prayer is that as you travel along with us, you will experience the same comfort and healing that we felt, but for your own unique situation.

I may not fully understand the why of all that we went through, but what I do know is this: If God's ultimate purpose for me were to live an easy and comfortable life, I would feel justified in shaking my fists at the heavens and blaming Him for completely abandoning us. But that is *not* His purpose for any of us. In fact, we are told the exact opposite as the Word of God promises tribulation (John 16:33), especially to those who are disciples of Christ (2 Timothy 3:12). We have been comforted with the instruction that Scripture provides regarding how we ought to *respond* in these circumstances (James 1:2-3) and how to find *purpose* in them (1 Peter 1:7).

PART II - JUDE

Discovery (March 7)

It was a seemingly typical spring afternoon when Juli went for a prenatal ultrasound. Due to August's complications, we were once again following the recommendations for more frequent testing for a high-risk pregnancy. My parents came over because my dad had to print something out from his email. I think my dad is the very last person to still have a Juno email account, which might explain his need for me to assist in such basic tasks like printing his emails. August and I were working on a puzzle on the living room floor, and I tried calling Juli as she was taking longer than usual. As more time passed, I began to grow impatient thinking that Juli decided to embark on her favorite hobby of driving from store to store returning things that she bought online that she never intended to keep anyway. My rarely anxious mind then thought that something bad must have happened since she was still not answering her phone. Was she in a car accident or did something happen at the appointment? I figured it was just my imagination, so I went outside to play with the kids in the backyard. As I pushed Augie in the swing, Juli finally answered.

She said that she was waiting for the doctor for a very long time. I stayed on the phone and Dr. Malik was on the other end of the phone using that tone of voice that you never wish to hear from a healthcare provider. She shared that the ultrasound revealed a minimal amount of amniotic fluid. She explained that since Juli's water had not broken yet, this was suggestive of a condition called bilateral renal agenesis, the technical term for a baby that does not develop any kidneys.

It was now time for an anatomy and physiology lesson. I never knew that the mother produces the amniotic fluid in early pregnancy, but this transitions to the baby producing the fluid later on in the pregnancy. In addition to the obvious issues with not having kidneys, the lack of amniotic fluid also hinders lung development so the prognosis was very poor with this particular diagnosis.

I sent the kids inside as I paced around in the backyard trying to process all that was being shared with me over the phone. Once we hung up, I had to go inside and give the kids a bath and figure out how to pretend like someone had not just told me that medically speaking, our baby was not going to live. Juli did end up having a few more errands to run, so I got the kids ready for bed and as we were eating dinner, I kept trying to process the reality of what I was just told. The kids were reading a new book and were claiming to be the different characters in the book. Wesley was the ninja. Dexter was the cowboy. Maggie was the bear. The new baby was the ping-pong ball (Don't ask me what kind of book we were reading, because I have no idea which book even has this random cast of characters). But would we ever get to meet that ping-pong ball? What were his chances of survival?

Juli came home and after putting the kids to bed, we discussed making plans for the recommended visit out to CHOP (Children's Hospital of Philadelphia) to confirm the diagnosis as well as when and how to tell the kids. We had plans to go snowboarding with my brother and his family that upcoming weekend, but we told them that our plans would have to be put on hold until we found out more. I also wondered how I could even begin to enjoy the simple pleasures of life like I once did knowing what we now knew. I was grateful as my brother offered to pray with us over the phone and offered to support us in any way that we needed.

As we laid awake in bed, we both knew that we were not going to get much sleep that night. This was by far the worst night of sleep either of us had ever had. We were not even sure what to say to one another so after we prayed, we both just laid there. I can't even remember what we talked about, but I think I remember trying to hold it all together and be the solid rock that my wife needed at that time. However, once she fell asleep after innumerable tears, my weeping started. I felt lost, broken, alone, even abandoned. I began to look up our son's diagnosis and desperately searched for potential treatments and chances of survival. I found that there was no standard of care for this, but that amnioinfusions (medically instilling fluid to replenish the loss of amniotic fluid) were often attempted as a clinical trial, but with very unpredictable and poor outcomes. As I sat there with my tear-stained face, the words to a song kept coming to mind…

"Magnify" by We are Messengers

I've been trying to make sense of the sorrow that I feel
Holding on for life to the only thing that's real…
My sight is incomplete and I made You look small
I've been staring at my problems for way too long
Realign where my hope is set
Until You're all that's left

God, be greater than the worries in my life
Be stronger than the weakness in my mind
Be louder, let Your glory come alive
Be magnified!

The Day Between Testing (March 8)

I went to work like any other weekday, but this day was unlike any I had experienced before. I went through the motions of my daily work responsibilities, but with my mind in a completely different place. My body was there but my brain was a thousand miles away in some sort of hazy, foggy land where I couldn't quite see clearly. Juli sent the kids off to school and arranged an appointment with CHOP for the very next morning. The plan was to get to CHOP by 6:30 a.m. so we had to leave by 4:45 a.m.

That morning, I was reading a commentary on Genesis by Ken Fleming regarding the faith of Abram. I couldn't help but relate in some way to the thoughts shared about a moment of weakness for Abram in Genesis 12 when he lied to Pharaoh in Egypt. "They compromised their faith in God by replacing it with fear. They missed out on experiencing how God would have provided for their needs in what seemed like impossible circumstance." Does this describe any particular moment in your life like it does ours?

The words to another song (written by a songwriter following her miscarriage) came to mind as a reminder of who is in control when life feels completely out of control.

"Thy Will" by Hillary Scott

I'm so confused
I know I heard You loud and clear
So I followed through
Somehow I ended up here
I don't wanna think
I may never understand
That my broken heart is a part of Your plan
When I try to pray
All I've got is hurt and these four words

Thy will be done

I know You're good
But this don't feel good right now
And I know You think
Of things I could never think about
It's hard to count it all joy
Distracted by the noise
Just trying to make sense
Of all Your promises

Sometimes I gotta stop
Remember that You're God
And I am not

Thy will be done

I told two coworkers about the ultrasound results and the need for follow-up testing at CHOP so I printed some forms for the next day's visit and headed home. I have no idea what happened at work that day. We tried to keep up with the normal routine of life, so I gave the boys haircuts and we spoke to the kids about our trip to the hospital to check-up on the baby. We had not yet told the kids the seriousness of the diagnosis as we first wanted to confirm what was seen at the previous visit. While we anxiously and nervously awaited the trip the next day, we asked for prayers from our family, church, and close friends:

"We would appreciate prayers for Juli and the baby. After a prenatal ultrasound last evening, we were given some pretty bad news and asked to follow-up at Children's Hospital of Philadelphia for a more definitive diagnosis. We are praying for better news and/or a miracle, but we know we are in His hands, and He is in control no matter what. It's a full day of testing tomorrow. Thank you so much for your prayers."

"You keep him in perfect peace whose mind is stayed on You."
–Isaiah 26:3

CHOP (March 9)

We woke up at 4:15 a.m. and drove to CHOP with our local Christian radio station on. It's amazing to see how the Lord tries to get our attention sometimes by hitting us from multiple angles. A friend texted me a few verses from Romans 8 and this local station was broadcasting a message about Romans 8, reminding the listener to trust in the Lord while "the Spirit helps in our weakness" (Romans 8:26). I needed these verses in this moment of weakness. Have you ever been brought to a Scripture from multiple sources and realized that God was trying to speak to you?

This idea of trusting in God in the midst of the storms of life was further brought to mind by one of Asaph's psalms:

21 Thus my heart was grieved,
And I was vexed in my mind.
22 I was so foolish and ignorant;
I was like a beast before You.
23 Nevertheless I am continually with You;
You hold me by my right hand.
24 You will guide me with Your counsel,
And afterward receive me to glory.
25 Whom have I in heaven but You?
And there is none upon earth that I desire besides You.
26 My flesh and my heart fail;
But God is the strength of my heart and my portion forever.
27 For indeed, those who are far from You shall perish;
You have destroyed all those who desert You for harlotry.
28 But it is good for me to draw near to God;
I have put my trust in the Lord GOD,
That I may declare all Your works.
–Psalm 73:21-28

I read these verses and prayed for strength that I might be a testimony to my wife and to the CHOP staff in what it means to trust in the Lord. We were brought into the ultrasound room from the waiting area, and they confirmed the very thing that we dreaded to hear. Our son had no evidence of kidneys in the ultrasound, which as they say in the medical community, is "not compatible with life." In this moment, our hearts and our flesh were failing, but we needed God as our strength and our portion (verse 26). We had no choice but to draw near to God and trust in Him as we were left feeling hopeless outside of His divine rule over our lives (verse 28).

As Juli was brought back for further testing, I hung out in the waiting area and made some phone calls to update our family. In describing to my dad that they could not visualize the kidneys, I also shared that due to the lack of urine production they were also unable to visualize the bladder. My dad understood the seriousness of not seeing any kidneys, but proceeded to ask, "How serious is the absence of a bladder? Is that a necessary organ?" With as much patience as I could muster for my health illiterate father (very wise, very literate, but not when it comes to healthcare), I responded, "Yes, dad, every person needs a bladder."

In all seriousness, my dad replied, "But I'm alive and they just removed my bladder last week."

"Dad…That was your *gall*bladder, not your *bladder.*" I needed a good laugh in that moment. Perhaps my dad really knew the difference, but perhaps the residual effects of eating a hardboiled egg (that he bought at a gas station and let sit in the car for a few hours before consuming) were also having an untoward effect on his cognition in addition to destroying his gallbladder.

I don't even remember what the results of the echocardiogram were, but Juli and I proceeded to meet with a genetic counselor to discuss our family history and then we had our final sit-down with the entire medical team. We entered the meeting with hopes that we were candidates for the clinical trial that appeared to be the only chance of survival for our baby. As they summarized their findings, they presented us with three options. We had the choice to:

1. Continue with the pregnancy until full term with no interventions.
2. "Interrupt" the pregnancy.
3. Participate in a clinical trial.

The second option was not a consideration for us for reasons that I will share later, but we were left with the decision to allow things to proceed naturally or join this clinical trial. When we arrived to CHOP early that morning, we were praying that we would be eligible as candidates to participate. With hopeful hearts, we rejoiced when they said we would be eligible to participate. However, as they walked us through the details of what was involved, we were faced with a difficult decision.

In order to participate, Juli would have to relocate to Philadelphia (within 15 minutes of CHOP) for the better part of the pregnancy due to the frequent "amnioinfusions" which would only become more frequent as the due date approached. She would need a family member to stay with her, which possibly meant our entire family temporarily relocating to Philly. This brought a number of different factors into this equation. What about the kids' school? What about my job? Even if Juli could get another family member to come up and stay with her, how would the kids manage without their mom for months on end (I was really asking how would *I* manage)?

What seemed to be an easy decision took a sudden turn in that brief meeting as we sat with the doctor, coordinator, and genetic counselor. The team was very sympathetic and understanding as we tried to formulate questions based on the information we were being given. In order to understand what we were trying to process I will try to summarize as briefly as possible what the team described to us. Due to the lack of kidneys, the amniotic fluid that would normally be produced by the baby's kidneys was no longer present. With the amnioinfusions, the medical team would infuse fluid into the amniotic sac. This is critical as the flow of amniotic fluid is essential in regard to the baby's lung development. Without this fluid, upon delivery, the baby would not be able to breathe on his own (or even with mechanical support).

If the lungs developed properly, the child would need to be on some form of dialysis for the first year of life. This would initially include months in the NICU and frequent admissions throughout the first year due to the increased likelihood of infection. If the baby survived long enough and grew to a size suitable for a kidney transplant, once a suitable donor was found, he would need to have bilateral kidney transplants and the necessary care for that (lifelong antirejection medications, etc.). When inquiring about the probability of survival without long-term debilitating conditions, they were unable to provide us with any statistics, but they shared that it was highly unlikely as CHOP had seen far more failures than successes in their time participating in this trial.

Crying in public or in group settings was not a common thing for our family, but we soon learned that this was going to be the beginning of many more open crying sessions. How grateful we were for the truth found in Psalm 56:8, "You have kept count of my tossings; put my tears in Your bottle. Are they not in Your book?" Our tears did not fall without our sovereign God taking notice.

I'm Not Crying, You're Crying

Since we had babysitters, we figured we would take advantage of it and enjoy (as much as we possibly could, given the current circumstances) a nice Italian lunch dinner at Maggiano's. The dreary weather matched our mood, and we figured what better way to lift our spirits than some fried zucchini sticks. Our favorite veggie appetizer did not disappoint, but the entrée continued to reinforce what we were feeling. I never send food back at a restaurant and if it wasn't for the events of the day I probably would have in this case. I enjoy chicken parmesan no matter where I order it from (including/especially from my hospital's cafeteria), but this was the coldest, chewiest, grayest chicken I had ever been served. I'm actually getting nauseous just writing about it.

We distracted ourselves from the meal by discussing our options and what would be the best decision. We talked in circles as we kept going back and forth between proceeding with the natural course of things or participating in this clinical trial. Our instinct was that we should do everything humanly possible to save our child. But what did that entail? What about the kids' education (we had homeschooled before), and what about my job (could I transition to fully remote)? Bigger questions continued to bombard us…

Should we do everything possible to prolong our son's life with no consideration of the quality of life? In discussing the clinical trial, the team shared with us that even if we participated, we needed to understand that this was not a clinically proven treatment for our son, but more or less "experimental." It was possible, if not likely, that the trial would not be successful. But did we not want to give our son that fighting chance? Would we feel instant regret as soon as he was born, thinking *If only we had done the trial*?

What impact would participation in the trial have on the growth and development of our other kids? What would the financial impact be? What would insurance cover? Obviously, we could never put a price on saving our child's life, but were we not loving our child if we didn't proceed with the trial? We would do anything possible to help or save our other children. Even looking back to all that we had gone through with August, we would have *never* considered withholding the necessary interventions. Why would we withhold treatment now even if there was a chance it would not work?

When we got home, we decided to sit down with the kids and tell them what the long visit to the hospital confirmed. Maggie and Wesley were in tears and our only daughter who had cried her heart out after finding out that she was going to have *yet another brother* just kept repeating, "I want a baby brother. I want a baby brother." We told Maggie that we needed to understand the reality of what the medical team had shared with us, but that we can, and we should pray for a miracle. Then came the question I was not prepared to answer.

"What if God's not real?" Maggie muttered through her sobbing.

In that moment, I didn't know how to respond to my 8-year-old who was obviously pondering more deeply than I had ever pondered at that age.

Lord, what do I say to her?

"Maggie, why do you say that?" I responded.

"We can pray for a miracle, but what if God doesn't save the baby?"

"Maggie…Just because God doesn't give us what we want or just because He doesn't answer our prayers the way we expect Him to, it doesn't mean that God is not real."

"Ok," she replied, still not fully satisfied with my response. It was a reminder to me that I would never have all the right answers, and that I could not instantly solve every concern that troubled my daughter's heart, but it did not mean that I wouldn't try.

"Maggie, feel your heartbeat…Listen to your breathing. What keeps your heart beating or your lungs breathing? You're not *telling* them to keep working. Even when you go to sleep, how do they keep going? God is with you even when we don't get what we want. Look how He took care of August. He can do it again if He chooses."

I laid in bed with Maggie trying to comfort her and realized that she had a lot on her mind, and she didn't need me to try to come up with the answers. She just wanted me to stay with her as she cried. After she fell asleep, I got up and shared with Juli how the conversation went. We knew we were heading into unknown territory, so we prayed for wisdom and strength to help carry our family through it.

I knew I needed to rely on God and His Word to survive and so I found myself in Acts 13. After reading this chapter, I really appreciated the thoughts from Dr. David Reid (from his 15-minute commentaries on each chapter of the Bible found on his website www.growingchristians.org – I highly recommend it if you are looking for great insight and practical application of the Word). He commented on the need for dependence on the Holy Spirit for direction. Just as Paul relied on the Spirit to lead him, we prayed for this same divine direction on how to navigate these upcoming months.

BREADCRUMBS

Now that you have a decent amount of background to our story, the rest of what you read will primarily be direct thoughts from my personal journal. Far gone are the days where I would have even attempted to write out my thoughts and feelings in a fancy private diary. My best attempt at processing my emotions was to save my half-thought-through thoughts in a note on my phone. It was more for my own personal coping, but I share them with you hoping that they will be an encouragement to someone who finds themself overcome with sorrow and unable to press on.

I share the following entries as evidence of God's sustaining hand over our lives. Some days He would give us breadcrumbs. Other days it would be a four-course meal. Either way, He never left us starving. Whereas we would have preferred a stockpile of endless food to sustain us through this emotional famine, like the children of Israel in the desert, we learned that our God would give us *exactly* what we needed (Exodus 16:16-18). Never lacking and never in excess, He provided for us in a way that sustained us yet kept us constantly trusting in Him.

My prayer is that you will read the thoughts below and find something relatable, whether it be a situation, a person, a conversation, a Bible verse, a song, a resource, or a comment. I pray that if you have ever thought, *"Yeah… that's me…I've been there,"* that you would find hope in the pages that follow.

Eight-Year-Old Wisdom (March 10)

We struggled with how much to share with our kids, especially when considering their various ages and stages of development. We shared more details about the clinical trial with Maggie thinking that she would like to know. After speaking to her the previous night, we were certain that her response would be for us to do everything that we possibly could to save her baby brother.

The next morning, however, Juli woke up to Maggie standing at her bedside saying, "I don't think we should do the trial." Our daughter went on to share that she believed that God knows everything before it happens and that maybe He knows something about our son's life that we don't. We were blown away by her wisdom, perspective and response.

Love, Hugs, and Prayers (March 10)

We went to our weekly prayer meeting at our chapel the next evening and we were met with a room filled with love. We realized that the baby's condition and poor prognosis was not easy to talk about. In fact, I realized that I would have found it extremely difficult to find the words to say to a friend who was in a similar situation. We shared the below update with our chapel family and had some wonderful conversations that night in between hugs and prayers:

"Thank you all for your prayers. After a long day at CHOP yesterday, it looks like they confirmed what they saw on Monday. The baby has something known as Potter's syndrome (rare defect where the baby does not have any kidneys). Prognosis is not good and there is no chance of survival outside of one experimental treatment which is very involved with unpredictable outcomes. We know God can work miracles, but we also continue to trust in the Lord in our current situation as we know His Plan and Purposes are Perfect."

"Whom have I in heaven but You? And there is none upon earth that I desire besides You. My flesh and my heart fail; But God is the strength of my heart and my portion forever. It is good for me to draw near to God; I have put my trust in the Lord God, that I may declare all Your works."
–Psalm 73:25-26, 28

What You Got in There? (March 11)

While it's true that "children are a gift from the Lord" (Psalm 127:3), they can also mess you up (in a good way). Today, Augie was talking with Juli and pointed at her belly and asked, "What you got in there?" Juli replied by telling him that his baby brother was in there to which he responded by affectionately rubbing her belly. Later on, we had friends visit with their newborn and our hearts broke as we saw how enthralled and captivated Augie was with this new little bundle of joy that came to visit. He was staring at this baby boy as we imagined him wondering in his little brain what an incredible big brother he would be one day. How are we supposed to hold it together with such awful cuteness in such an awful situation? We were learning that tears of joy and sorrow both had healing powers, each in their own way.

So Many Questions (March 12)

We decided to go on our planned snowboarding trip to north Jersey. Juli hung out in the lodge as August explored the new sights and sounds of a "ski resort" (I use the term loosely) for the first time. I was on the very small mountain with the kids reminding myself that despite the overwhelming weight of the sorrow in my heart, it was good for us to be there to make these memories with our children. It was so hard thinking that we wouldn't be able to make these memories with the newest member of our family. I would never get to teach him how to snowboard. I would never get the chance to remind him that no matter how many times you fall, you have to always choose to get back up again. We were exhausted by the time we got back to the hotel, but after a few trips up and down the "mountain" (again, I use the term loosely) and exploring the woods behind the lodge, we were ready for a good night's rest. The hotel manager actually gave us an additional room, so Jim and Lisa had their room, Juli and I had ours (with August), and the kids got their own "party room." Since we forgot the portable baby crib, August slept in our bed for the first time ever and we had no problem with it whatsoever. We were just going to enjoy being with him and he enjoyed being with us. Or perhaps he simply enjoyed the fact that we let him stay up and watch cartoons until 1 in the morning. At this point, we didn't care. We said our "I love yous" as we pointed at Augie's eye and he finished the phrase and said goodnight.

I laid awake in bed and began to read an online article about an author that a friend had shared with me. Her name was Angie Smith and she had gone through something very similar to what we were going through. I decided that it would be helpful for us to read this to gain a better understanding of how she navigated through the daily tears and heartache if we were beginning the long journey ourselves.

When Juli woke up the next morning, we realized that the pain was going to hit us in a new way each and every day. We both would often wake up and think that this awful diagnosis was just a miserably terrible dream, only having to remember over and over again every morning that this was our reality. We were learning new depths of sadness that we had never known before.

On our way home, we stopped by the American Dream Mall, a 3 million square foot madhouse with more stimuli than any one person can handle. While we were walking through Old Navy and the kids were playing hopscotch in the aisle, Juli and I both choked up as we walked past the baby pajamas at the back of the store. Was this what it was going to be like for the next six months? Or even longer? Every little thing reminding us of the baby that medical professionals said we would never have a chance to nurture.

After we got home, I quickly changed and headed out to a funeral for one of my dad's close friends. This took more of an emotional toll on me than I had anticipated. As we sang the hymn "It is Well with My Soul," I was reminded of the peace that God provides in the heaviest of storms:

When peace like a river attendeth my way
When sorrows like sea billows roll
Whatever my lot, though has taught me to say
It is well, It is well with my soul

A couple with whom we served as youth group leaders with for many years comforted us through their love and hugs as we spoke after the funeral. Other friends who we had not seen in a while and were not aware of our situation asked the typical "How are the kids doing?"

…How do you answer that?… *"The kids are fine except the one that we haven't met yet, he's already got an expiration date."*

How much do we share with people? Would we be known as the "downers" that no one wanted around because we would just kill the mood of every room we entered? We didn't want to make others feel uncomfortable with our presence or for others to not feel like they could talk about happy things happening in their lives. How much should we open up and share with people? Did that depend on how close we were with them or how long the conversation would go? So many questions. We are still trying to figure this whole thing out.

Still Tough (March 13)

Our first Sunday morning back at church was a good one, but a tough one. Hugs from everyone. My friend Alan gave the best hug as he nearly crushed me with his strength, but it reminded me that he was there for me. During the morning meeting, a few of our kids would stand next to Juli and hug her belly. Tough to think that there was a time limit to how often they might get to hug their baby brother. Conversations were still tough. Our niece asked if there was a baby inside of Aunt Juli's belly to which Dexter responded, "Yes, but he's going to be born and stay with us and die and go to heaven." Very matter of fact, but incredibly difficult for me to hear that and truly process it myself, let alone understand what my four-year-old is trying to process.

At this point, I had already heard the song by Katy Nichole entitled "In Jesus' Name" (in fact, I believe it was as we were on our drive home from CHOP). While the lyrics taught me to pray with more faith and without doubting (James 1:6), I kept asking myself about the times that God chooses to not answer our prayers in the way we so desperately want him to.

I pray for your healing, that circumstances would change
I pray that a breakthrough would happen today
I pray miracles over your life in Jesus' name
I pray that the dead will come to life in Jesus' name

What if our circumstances don't change? What if God doesn't miraculously heal our son? What if we don't receive the breakthrough we are praying for? The music video for this song reminded me that God may not always answer our prayers in the way that we expect, but we believe He answers in so many other ways as He drew us together as a single family unit dependent on Him. This was expressed in the music video as a family was portrayed driving home from the hospital after losing their child. Despite the tragedy, the family is carried through this deep sorrow:

"In Jesus' Name" by Katy Nichole

I speak the name of Jesus over you
In your hurting, in your sorrow
I will ask my God to move
I speak the name 'cause it's all that I can do
In desperation, I'll seek Heaven
And pray this for you

I pray for your healing, that circumstances would change
I pray that the fear inside would flee in Jesus' name
I pray that a breakthrough would happen today
I pray miracles over your life in Jesus' name
In Jesus' name

I speak the name of all authority
Declaring blessings, every promise
He is faithful to keep
I speak the name no grave could ever hold
He is greater, He is stronger
He's the God of possible

Come believe it, come receive it
Oh, the power of His Spirit is now forever yours
Come believe it, come receive it
In the mighty name of Jesus, all things are possible

I pray for your healing, that circumstances will change
I pray that the fear inside would flee in Jesus' name
I pray that a breakthrough would happen today
I pray miracles over your life in Jesus' name
I pray for revival, for restoration of faith
I pray that the dead will come to life in Jesus' name
In Jesus' name

Unless Your Law Had Been My Delight (March 14)

It's been one week since we were given the diagnosis for our son. It's hard to believe that one week ago we were joyfully expecting a healthy baby boy. Mentally, I'm in a completely different place right now. I told my bosses about our situation, and they let me work from home for the rest of the week. That's all good and well, but how can I even fulfill my work responsibilities with this diagnosis weighing so heavily on me? I spoke with a friend in our driveway who shared about his sister's loss of a child and the sorrow that their family faced. We would never rejoice in another family's sorrow, but it's comforting to know that God has carried other families through tremendous loss.

My friend gave me a hug and it struck me that I was incredibly grateful that we were not going through this stage of life during the COVID-19 pandemic. Perhaps it's the Italian side of me, but I don't think I would have survived if I did not have the opportunity to be embraced and covered by the love of friends and family. How tough it must have been for those who lost loved ones during the height of the quarantine where social distancing was often mandated and family gatherings, even funerals, were often forbidden.

Later that day, I spoke with my friend Max on the phone who shared a Bible verse that, unbeknownst to me, would forever change how God would carry me through this.

"Unless Your law had been my delight, I would then have perished in my affliction."
–Psalm 119:92

I could not, in my affliction, *neglect* the Word of God. I had to learn to *delight* in it. Max sent me a message from Mike Attwood reminding us that "Defeat should not be the default position for believers." This was a message about growing complacent in a life characterized by consistent failure and falling into sin, but what about me? What about losing hope, feeling depressed, allowing sorrow to consume me? Was this sin? Grieving is necessary, but if it causes me to lose hope in Christ, to *me* it becomes sin. Grieving should cause us to fall helplessly into the arms of Christ (thinking of the lyrics to *Come What May* by We Are Messengers). Mike went on to say that a day that we do not allow Christ to live and love through us is a wasted day. Reminder: Begin every day with a vote of *no confidence in the flesh*.

Juli just shared with me how she was thinking about a family that recently visited our chapel and that the last time we saw her they shared how they would be having babies around the same time. We knew random memories would creep up slowly or pop into our minds suddenly and we had to be ready for waves of emotion to come and go. She brought Maggie to softball practice and ran into a friend while grabbing some ice cream and was able to share a conversation and a hug as she shared our news. We realized that we would have a lot of these conversations and hoped that it would get easier with time.

While Juli was out with Maggie, Dexter and Wesley fell asleep. Augie was refusing to go to bed, so I picked him up and we danced in the living room. I cherished every hug and began to cry as he laid his head on me. This is what memories are made of…then he fell down and split his lip open…these are also memories.

Juli and I watched a movie called the *Adam Project* and the concept was about a character going back in time and visiting a younger version of himself. I was wondering if watching movies would become our way of escaping the depressing reality that was hovering like a dark cloud over our lives now. But then the movie ended with the younger character playing catch in the backyard with this older version of himself, when he suddenly disappears. The tears started flowing as I thought how I may never get the chance to throw a baseball with our son. As I lay in bed fighting back the tears, I eventually wrote a letter to Jude (I think at this time we had settled on a name) to thank him for the change he had already made in my own heart. I would eventually share this letter at Jude's memorial service.

Joy (March 15)

Would I ever be able to truly experience joy in this life again?

"Joy is a quiet gladness of heart as one contemplates the goodness of God's saving grace in Christ Jesus."
–John Calvin

Hugs (March 16)

I just so happened to be on our front porch while attending our hospital's virtual daily safety huddle, when my friend Mike from down the street drove by on his way to work. He was rushing to work, but hopped out and gave me a giant hug. This was the first time I was seeing him since we got the news. That's all I remember, but that's all that matters. Did I mention that I love hugs? These displays of affection from loved ones are helping me get through the tough times.

Issues (March 17)

Juli is a pretty good listener. In fact, compared to me, she is an incredibly awesome listener and would often be the one to let friends and family pour out their hearts and share their daily struggles. I love this about her (among many other things). However, I could see the dilemma she faced as she tried to cope with our son's diagnosis while at the same time giving her best attempts at comforting those who came to her to share their personal issues.

It was becoming more and more difficult to listen to people vent about their frustrations of their baby not sleeping or their kid being a handful. At least they have a baby that is keeping them up at night. At least their kid was alive and well enough to be giving them a hard time. Our natural response was to become annoyed at the lack of consideration. Do you even realize what you're complaining about? We would love to have the problems you're having and not the one we currently had.

Juli and I had to do some soul-searching as we sat and tried to put ourselves in someone else's shoes. Would it have been wrong to ask our friends and family to not come to us any more with their petty issues? Probably not, but we had to think back to a time when our biggest issue in life was when Maggie was born, and she refused to eat for what felt like an entire year. Even though Maggie was a poor feeder, she was still getting the nutrients she needed (just barely). This was our biggest concern eight years ago. In fact, life was pretty easy come to think of it up until everything we went through with August. We reminded ourselves that those early days with Maggie were the hardest thing we had dealt with up until that point in our lives and so we asked for strength to continue to have the same compassion on others as many had already shown toward us. Was it hard? Yes. Did we sometimes have to ask loved ones to not come to us with their problems? Yes. Actually, most people went to Juli, so we tried to find a loving way of asking others to bring their problems elsewhere for the time being.

We sometimes felt like we needed a place to hide. Psalm 32:7 reminded us of where we needed to go:

"You are my hiding place;
You shall preserve me from trouble;
You shall surround me with songs of deliverance."
–Psalm 32:7

Did *Your* Baby Die? (March 18)

Juli brought Dexter to drop a present off for a friend's baby. As Juli shared with Dexter about the arrival of his friend Maria's baby sister, he innocently asked, "Is she dead?" That was all that he could process concerning new babies with his baby brother's diagnosis perhaps consuming his little mind. He responded with disbelief and frustration when Juli told him that the baby was not dead. My wife explained to Dexter that the baby was alive and well and that we should thank the Lord for that. When they arrived, Maria ran down to the end of the driveway and told Dexter that she had a new baby sister. Dexter handed Maria a present and in a very matter-of-fact manner said, "My baby is dead." Juli was speechless. She can't even recall how that conversation continued, but she was grateful that her sunglasses hid the tears that began to flow. When they drove away, Juli once again had to explain to Dexter that his baby brother was not dead, but alive and safe in mommy's belly, but someday soon he might go to heaven to be with Jesus. First of all, what kind of four-year-old says these kinds of things? Secondly, why would he get so frustrated? Perhaps I will never understand the thought processes of a four-year-old and perhaps that's a good thing.

Juli had to explain to Dexter that just because we are being told that something is likely to happen to our baby doesn't mean that we wish that upon others. She called me in tears as she was trying to process her own grieving as well as the complex mind of our son, whose comments didn't make things any easier. My coworker stepped out of our office to provide privacy as I worked through this conversation with Juli (so thankful for my awesome coworkers). I'm reminded of Matthew 5:4, "Blessed are those who mourn, for they will be comforted."

Lord, please comfort Juli. Please help me to comfort her. Please comfort me.

Living in the Land of Death (March 19)

How can we keep pressing on through the darkness?

"If God promised to hold the hand of the Messiah, you can be sure He will hold the hands of the Messiah's disciples."
–Paul Washer

"In heaven, God is boasting of you…Look at My servant who walks in darkness and yet trusts in My Name."
–Paul Washer

My friend Mike sent me a song called *Fires* by Jordan St. Cyr and the music video shows individuals and families that the Lord walked with through their own personal "fires." As I read more of the personal testimony of this artist, he shared about his daughter who has been in and out of the hospital with seizures and a complex medical history with an unknown outcome. These lyrics hit me hard (as well as the ones further below from Citizens):

"Fires" by Jordan St. Cyr

I remember how You told me, That life may not be easy
And everything that I need, You've already given me
I remember how You told me, I can trust You completely
So why am I doubting, When You proved that You'd fight for me

You've walked me through fires, Pulled me from flames
If You're in this with me, I won't be afraid
When the smoke billows higher, oh and higher
And it feels like I can barely breathe
I'll walk through these fires, 'Cause You're walking with me

I'm changed by Your mercy, Covered by Your peace
I'm living out the victory, Doesn't mean I won't feel the heat

You've walked me through fires, Pulled me from flames
If You're in this with me, I won't be afraid
When the smoke billows higher, oh and higher
And it feels like I can barely breathe
I'll walk through these fires, 'Cause You're walking with me

I can face anything (Anything)
'Cause You're here with me (Here with me)
I can do all things (Do all things)
'Cause You strengthen me

I remember how You showed me, The price of my redemption
Lord, how could I question, When You proved that You'd die for me

"I am Living in a Land of Death" by Citizens

I'm living in a land of death
The trees are burning grey
There's a smoldering smoke overhead
And the night looks the same as the day
It seems a miracle that I can stand
When everyone I've known
Drifts up in the air with the ash

Every time that the wind starts to blow

But I feel alive with a life that's not mine
Your law is a stream in this wasteland, my lifeline
So much more than precious gold
Are Your promises my Lord
By them is Your servant warned
In keeping them great reward

Your direction is marked in light
Your law secures my wounds
I will meditate day and night
And in season You'll harvest Your fruit
Though a poison should threaten to kill
I know my Savior reigns
And when the breezes of death leave a chill
I've got Jesus' blood in my veins

So I feel alive with a life that's not mine
And I'm believing that, that was Your intended design
So much more than precious gold
Are Your promises, my Lord
By them is Your servant warned
In keeping them great reward

Revive Me Again (March 20)

In our Lord's Supper service this morning, as we remembered the sacrifice of our Savior, Psalm 71 was read, and I could not stop reading it over and over again to myself and hearing God speak directly to me. I was asked how I was doing personally which was a reminder that our church family was praying for all of us, for Juli, Maggie, Wesley, Dexter, August, and even me. It's so humbling to know that others are lifting up our needs before an Almighty God who is able to answer the prayers that we cry out to Him like the ones found in this psalm.

Psalm 71

In You, O LORD, I put my trust;
Let me never be put to shame.
² Deliver me in Your righteousness, and cause me to escape;
Incline Your ear to me, and save me.
³ Be my strong refuge,
To which I may resort continually;

You have given the commandment to save me,
For You are my rock and my fortress.
⁴ Deliver me, O my God, out of the hand of the wicked,
Out of the hand of the unrighteous and cruel man.
⁵ For You are my hope, O Lord GOD;
You are my trust from my youth.
⁶ By You I have been upheld from birth;
You are He who took me out of my mother's womb.
My praise shall be continually of You.
⁷ I have become as a wonder to many,
But You are my strong refuge.
⁸ Let my mouth be filled with Your praise
And with Your glory all the day.
⁹ Do not cast me off in the time of old age;
Do not forsake me when my strength fails.
¹⁰ For my enemies speak against me;
And those who lie in wait for my life take counsel together,
¹¹ Saying, "God has forsaken him;
Pursue and take him, for there is none to deliver him."
¹² O God, do not be far from me;
O my God, make haste to help me!
¹³ Let them be confounded and consumed
Who are adversaries of my life;
Let them be covered with reproach and dishonor
Who seek my hurt.
¹⁴ But I will hope continually,
And will praise You yet more and more.
¹⁵ My mouth shall tell of Your righteousness
And Your salvation all the day,
For I do not know their limits.
¹⁶ I will go in the strength of the Lord GOD;
I will make mention of Your righteousness, of Yours only.
¹⁷ O God, You have taught me from my youth;
And to this day I declare Your wondrous works.
¹⁸ Now also when *I* am old and grayheaded,
O God, do not forsake me,
Until I declare Your strength to this generation,
Your power to everyone who is to come.
¹⁹ Also Your righteousness, O God, is very high,
You who have done great things;
O God, who is like You?
²⁰ You, who have shown me great and severe troubles,
Shall revive me again,
And bring me up again from the depths of the earth.

²¹ You shall increase my greatness,
And comfort me on every side.
²² Also with the lute I will praise You—
And Your faithfulness, O my God!
To You I will sing with the harp,
O Holy One of Israel.
²³ My lips shall greatly rejoice when I sing to You,
And my soul, which You have redeemed.
²⁴ My tongue also shall talk of Your righteousness all the day long;
For they are confounded,
For they are brought to shame
Who seek my hurt.

Just a Dream… (March 21)

I woke up in a panic and sweat as I dreamt of the day of Jude's delivery. I felt helpless and confused. I was frustrated with myself for not choosing to do the clinical trial and found myself helpless in not being able to do anything to save my son. I remembered Psalm 71:3, "Be my strong refuge to which I may resort continually. You have given the commandments to save me, for You are my rock and my fortress."

Maggie and Wesley were talking to their Spanish teacher at school and Wesley shared with Juli that he started to cry as he began to talk to his teacher about his baby brother. How could we learn to comfort our children when we couldn't even comfort ourselves? The Scriptures that my heart was drawn to and the testimony of others gave us the strength to press on. I continued to learn more about the daughter of Jordan St. Cyr, the artist that I mentioned two days ago. The video he shared was one of how God helped him and his family through the pain and suffering of caring for their sick daughter. I began to listen to his entire album which seemed like God had caused him to write it for me as I reflected on the words in one of his other songs:

"Let Go, Let God" by Jordan St. Cyr

I tried to make this better
It didn't go so well
Some things in life I can't make right all by myself
Seems like an uphill battle
Feels like it's just no fair
Some things in life I can't make right but even then I've gotta

Let go and let God put me back together
I don't think I can live like this forever

I've only got two hands
I can't hold the world but He can
I know I've got to let go and let God

Why don't I just surrender
I run from it every time
Don't I believe He's all I need even when I
Feel like I'm treading water
Fighting for every breath
Don't I believe He's all I need
He'll give me rest when I

Let go and let God put me back together
I don't think I can live like this forever
I've only got two hands
I can't hold the world but He can
I know I've got to let go and let God

Let God, Be my rest, be my peace, be my healing
Let God, Be my joy, be my life, be my freedom
Oh God, You're my rest, You're my peace, You're my healing
My God, You're my joy, You're my life, You're my freedom

The kids continue to pray for Jude every time we sit and pray as a family. Juli also just started feeling the baby kick. I had more eagerness to feel these kicks than any other pregnancy as I wasn't sure if these would be the only interactions with my son, but it was still too early for anyone but Juli to feel anything. I'm really looking forward to it.

Then this verse hit me right when I needed it. Thank you, God.

"Therefore, the redeemed of the LORD shall return and come with singing unto Zion; and everlasting joy shall be upon their head; they shall obtain gladness and joy. Sorrow and mourning shall flee away."
–Isaiah 51:11

Better than Life (March 22)

Can I consider our knowledge of the eventual but imminent loss of our son as a gift from God, as a demonstration of His grace? Without this knowledge, we would not have leaned on God so heavily. The family of God would not have had as much of an opportunity to "weep with those who weep" and thus fulfill the Scriptures (Romans 12:15). As a recently popular Disney song puts it, "We've heard how big the iceberg is and we are not swerving." This foreknowledge is a gift that has allowed us to depend on a much more reliable source of life than ourselves…the Giver of Life Himself.

"Your love is better than life."
–Psalm 63:3

How can anything prove to be better than life? God's love and grace has allowed us to love this child as he is formed in the womb. We have learned to love his little kicks more than we have appreciated each of the other pregnancies as we realize outside of a miracle, we have a solid 20 weeks to love him. At the end of the night, I had the privilege of connecting with my friend Scott who recently lost his son. As he prayed with me over the phone, I thanked God for him and his encouragement to me in that moment and just thought: This guy is awesome, and I needed that.

…Or a Nightmare? (March 23)

I woke up from another dream of the delivery day. This is not easy. We had an ultrasound appointment at the new location at the mall and it got me thinking…*Are we just going through the motions of a normal pregnancy when this is anything but normal?* It was difficult to hear them say that the growth and development was right on track. Difficult to see and hear a strong healthy heart and know that he might not survive long after delivery. At CHOP, they shared that they did not see any sign of kidneys, but today, we were told they saw something that might resemble a kidney? Could this be the start of a miracle? We had never prayed as sincerely for anything else in our lives before this and was God in the process of performing the impossible? They shared with us that due to the fact that there was still no amniotic fluid that even if it were a kidney, it was not functioning. The neonatologist shared that Juli very likely could go to full term before delivering. We asked about organ donation thinking that if Jude had other healthy organs or tissue, why not help another baby in need.

I thought about 1 Thessalonians 4:13 today, "But I do not want you to be ignorant, brethren, concerning those who have fallen asleep, lest you sorrow as others who have no hope." We had never experienced sorrow like this before, but we were reminded that while our sorrow is real, it's different. It's not a hopeless sorrow. It's a sorrow that is surrounded by the promises found in God's Word. Reminders of the hope that we have keep coming up in so many of the songs that we've been listening to, some of which I have already shared (and some of which I will share later), but Dexter keeps asking to listen to these songs and we are finding that each time we listen, we are reminded of that wonderful hope.

Through Waters, Rivers, and Fire (March 24)

"When you pass through the waters, I will be with you; And through the rivers, they shall not overflow you. When you walk through the fire, you shall not be burned, nor shall the flame scorch you."
–Isaiah 43:2

Birth Plan (March 29)

"But You, O LORD, are a shield for me; my glory and the One who lifts up my head."
–Psalm 3:3

I spoke with Susan, who oversees Pediatric Palliative Care at the hospital where I work. I shared with her about CHOP suggesting we come out there for delivery, but I am often reminded of the great reputation that this program at Monmouth Medical Center had. We spoke about a birth plan and what type of support might be needed throughout the pregnancy and after delivery. I mentioned about how I am looking forward to holding our son's hand and praying that even if he doesn't stay with us long, that I would be able to feel him squeeze my finger. I keep getting emotionally overwhelmed. I was able to share how our faith is getting us through this and that it was not the strength of our faith, but the strength of the God whom we are putting our faith in.

I called Max back after missing a call from him. He always has the perfect verse to share on the days that I need it the most.

"How precious also are Your thoughts to me, O God! How great is the sum of them!"
–Psalm 139:17

Pour Out Your Grief (March 30)

"Hear me when I call, O God of my righteousness! You have relieved me in my distress; Have mercy on me and hear my prayer."
–Psalm 4:1

"But as for me, I will come into Your house in the multitude of Your mercy; in fear of You I will worship toward Your holy temple."
–Psalm 5:7

"What is the reason for your depression? The loss of a child? Pour out your grief to God. Ask your friends to help share your grief with you. And realize

that life is not over for you. The best testimony of your love for that person is to go on and live a life in their honor for God's glory."
–I cannot remember where I read this, but it is immensely helpful.

"Look inward and analyze your heart. Then, look upward and recognize your Help."
–Also, I can't remember where I read this, but I needed it.

"God will give me grace in this trial to behave like His child."
–I can't remember who said this either…

Surrounded (March 31)

"In this valley, we have absolutely felt surrounded by love. That's what the body of Christ should feel like…He will never leave us or forsake us."
–Toby Mac (in sharing about the sudden and tragic death of his son)

We have felt the same sort of love surrounding us from family, friends, and the body of Christ.

I Am Weak (April 1)

"But let all those rejoice who put their trust in You; let them ever shout for joy, because You defend them; Let those also who love Your name be joyful in You."
–Psalm 5:11

"Have mercy on me, O LORD, for I am weak; O LORD, heal me, for my bones are troubled."
–Psalm 6:2

Faithfully Pray (April 3)

"I will praise the LORD according to His righteousness,
And will sing praise to the name of the LORD Most High."
–Psalm 7:17

The kids wonderfully and faithfully pray for a miracle for their baby brother. What an example to Juli and me!

Providence (April 5)

"The amazing thing about God's providence from *our* perspective is that we only see it in hindsight. We cannot see God's providence looking from here to

tomorrow, but from here to yesterday."
–Voddie Baucham

Dexter was riding in the car with Juli today and as they drove past a cemetery, he asked if Jude was in there. There are times when the cares of this world distract me from our present reality, but the kids often bring me back. I find myself physically present, but a thousand miles away. Lost in thought…or disbelief…or pain. I can't quite figure out what it is yet.

"For our light affliction, which is but for a moment, is working for us a far more exceeding and eternal weight of glory."
–2 Corinthians 4:17

Work Support (April 7)

I went up to a former department that I covered in my nursing education days and saw some old friends. I got a hug from a coworker, Amanda, who had recently gone through the loss of a child, and it was exactly what I needed. The reality of what we were going through hit me hard at that moment. I wanted to speak with her privately, but nurses have to do what nurses have to do and she was soon running off to her next task. I sent her a text to say thank you for the embrace and asked her if we could connect later.

I called another coworker, Carolyn, who was currently working in our hospital's PMAD (Perinatal Mood & Anxiety Disorder) department to discuss what services they offered. I didn't feel as if Juli was currently going through any sort of crisis, but I thought that it might be helpful to see what services and support they offered. It was a comforting conversation. I shared that Juli had a great support network and there was no better support than what we were currently getting from our loved ones, friends, and church family. My coworker mentioned that many people bring their personal faith along with them as a source of hope and comfort while receiving professional support services.

Breakfast of Champions (April 9)

While attending our chapel's monthly Men & Boys Prayer Breakfast, Dr. Terry Gilpin shared the perfect devotional that highlighted an often-repeated phrase found in Scripture that was exactly what I needed to hear.

…Be of good cheer…

"Then behold, they brought to Him a paralytic lying on a bed. When Jesus saw their faith, He said to the paralytic, 'Son, be of good cheer; your sins are forgiven you.'"
–Matthew 9:2

Be of good cheer when reminded of *past* sins forgiven.

"But immediately Jesus spoke to them, saying, 'Be of good cheer! It is I; do not be afraid.'" –Matthew 14:27

Be of good cheer because of the confidence of Jesus' *present* comfort in the midst of the storm.

"These things I have spoken to you, that in Me you may have peace. In the world, you will have tribulation; but be of good cheer, I have overcome the world." –John 16:33

Be of good cheer because of the promise of *future* peace despite known troubles ahead.

I finally did get a chance to call that coworker that I ran into the other day. Despite having different personal trials, she provided the tremendously helpful reminder that God has a plan and can often show His grace towards us in ways we would never expect.

The Wisdom of Wesley (April 12)

Wesley prayed today, "We pray for a miracle, but even if we don't get one, we pray that we would still worship God." Can I realistically do this? I want to say yes, but it's been especially difficult.

Another truth from my coworker I just spoke with, "Sometimes God shows us His grace by not giving us what we want." This was something she learned through her experience. I'm praying for the strength to honestly see this same truth.

From My Dear Friend Max (April 13)

Max has been such a blessing with the encouragement that he sends my way as seen in the below collection of verses and reflections:

"We do not have a high priest who is unable to sympathize with our weaknesses, but one who in every respect has been tempted as we are, yet without sin" (Hebrews 4:15). I have never heard anyone say, "The really deep lessons of my life have come through times of ease and comfort." But I have heard strong saints say, "Every significant advance I have ever made in grasping the depths of God's love and growing deep with him, has come through suffering." This is a sobering biblical truth. For example: "For Christ's sake I have suffered the loss of all things and count them as rubbish, in order that I may gain Christ" (Philippians 3:8). Paraphrase: No pain, no gain. Now let it all be sacrificed, if it will get me more of Christ.

Here's another example: "Although he was a Son, Jesus learned obedience through what he suffered" (Hebrews 5:8). The same book said he never sinned (Hebrews 4:15). So, learning obedience does not mean switching from disobedience to obedience. It means growing deeper and deeper with God in the experience of obedience. It means experiencing the possible depths of yielding to God that would not have been otherwise attained. This is what came through suffering. No pain, no gain.

Samuel Rutherford said that when he was cast into the cellars of affliction, he remembered that the great king always kept his wine there. Charles Spurgeon said, "They who dive in the sea of affliction bring up rare pearls." Do you not love your beloved more when you feel some strange pain that makes you think you have cancer? We are strange creatures indeed. If we have health and peace and time to love, it can become a thin and hasty thing. But if we are dying, love becomes a deep, slow river of inexpressible joy, and we can scarcely endure to give it up. Therefore, brothers and sisters, "Count it all joy when you meet trials of various kinds" (James 1:2).

Thanks, Max.

The Sacred Dance (April 14)

"As your days, so shall your strength be."
–Deuteronomy 33:25b

I started reading Angie Smith's book *I Will Carry You: The Sacred Dance of Grief and Joy.* This book that was recommended by my friend, Craig, was especially relatable as I found how incredibly similar our stories were. Both Angie's family and our family had dealt with the loss of a baby (miscarriage for Angie, ectopic pregnancy for Juli), followed by healthy children, and then the next child with an ultrasound revealing some bad news. "In the days after Audrey was diagnosed, I began to see Scripture with new eyes. I was desperate for truth in the midst of the chaos. I began to search for stories of healing in hopes of peace" (Smith, 2010, p. 23).

It was equally true for me. Same Scriptures. New perspective. Many friends shared verses that I knew, but they hit me in a different way. Our friend, Meghan, shared the above verse reminding us that God would provide the strength we needed for each day. Max reminded me of Luke 22:32, "But I have prayed for you, that your faith should not fail; and when you have returned to Me, strengthen your brethren."

"Lord, behold, he whom You love is sick."
–John 11:3.

Smith (2010) walked her readers through the story of Lazarus, and we know that the same love that our Savior had for Lazarus, He has for our son now.

Sense & Sensitivity (April 16)

We took a family trip down to visit Juli's family in Florida. At an Easter egg hunt at their chapel, some of Juli's friends opened up and shared the emotional ups and downs through many years of multiple miscarriages. One friend shared how she learned to honestly share her emotions with God. As I shared my experience, we marveled at the rawness of the emotions spoken to God by many of the psalmists. While many sympathized with what we were going through, we also realized this was a personal situation that we had not broadcasted widely for everyone's awareness. This reality hit hard as some friends who were unaware of our son's diagnosis made jokes about the pregnancy that they otherwise would not have had they known the situation. We learned to be gracious, just as we would appreciate the same response toward us if we had been unknowingly insensitive to another's situation.

"Behold, I tell you a mystery: We shall not all sleep, but we shall all be changed – in a moment, in the twinkling of an eye, at the last trumpet. For the trumpet will sound, and the dead will be raised incorruptible, and we shall be changed. For this corruptible must put on incorruption, and this mortal must put on immortality. So, when this corruptible has put on incorruption, and this mortal has put on immortality, then shall be brought to pass the saying that is written:

'Death is swallowed up in victory.'
'O Death, where is your sting?'
'O Hades, where is your victory?'

The sting of death is sin, and the strength of sin is the law. But thanks be to God, who gives us the victory through our Lord Jesus Christ. Therefore, my beloved brethren, be steadfast, immovable, always abounding in the work of the Lord, knowing that your labor is not in vain in the Lord."
–1 Corinthians 15:51-58

Changing Minds (April 19)

Does God really "change His mind?" Some would argue that a number of passages suggest that this is indeed the case where God hears the prayers of His saints and changes His mind. We see that Abraham pleaded with God and God heard Him. In the famous battle where the sun stood still at Joshua's request, we read, "And there has been no day like that, before it or after it, that the Lord heeded the voice of a man; for the Lord fought for Israel" (Joshua 10:14). When Hezekiah pleaded with God that he would be delivered from his fatal illness, God heard him, and Isaiah proclaimed that God would extend his life.

Is this the same kind of faith that we pray with? Is this the same kind of God that we believe in?

In Angie Smith's reflection of the resurrection of Lazarus, Jesus was not saying that Mary and Martha's faith enabled Him to perform the miracle, but rather that it allowed them to see the glory of God.

"I believe that everything that happens in our lives, however awful, is an opportunity to bring glory to Jesus. Have I wished it had been in a different way? Of course, I do. And you probably do, too. If I choose to, I can hold that against Him. I can let it embitter me for the rest of my days, as I walk around finding holes in everything He has done. All of us have times of crisis. The most we can do is accept what happens next with the grace that says circumstances will define neither God's love for us nor our love for God" (Smith, 2010, p. 119).

For His Name's Sake (April 20)

"He restores my soul; He leads me in the paths of righteousness for His name's sake."
–Psalm 23:3

Other translations will say that He *refreshes* or *repairs* my soul.

Lord, we need this restoration.

This Path, Too? (April 21)

"Lead me in Your truth and teach me, for you are the God of my salvation; on You I wait all the day. All the paths of the Lord are mercy and truth, to such as keep His covenant and His testimonies. Turn Yourself to me and have mercy on me, for I am desolate and afflicted."
–Psalm 25:5, 10, 16

All of the paths? Even this one? Lord, teach me to wait patiently on You.

Baby Brother (April 23)

As we began our drive from Florida back to New Jersey, we were sending Juli's second cousin, Jude, a birthday message over the phone in the car and Maggie said, "Let's make him a cupcake for when he visits." Dexter yelled out, "No! We can't because he won't be alive." In his typical, matter-of-fact manner, he was freely speaking what his heart was feeling as he imagined this cupcake being made for his yet-to-be-born brother, Jude.

We got home and arrived to find that our neighbor, Abbey, had left an ultrasound device on our porch so that we could hear the baby's heartbeat with the kids. We were praying for her baby who had some major upcoming surgeries. There were constant reminders that we were not the only ones going through difficult times. May our prayers be focused on His will being worked out in the lives of everyone around us, including us.

King Forever (April 26)

"The Lord sat enthroned at the flood, and the Lord sits as king forever."
–Psalm 29:10

We began to arrange meetings with the Pediatric Palliative Care team at MMC and needed to start writing down some questions to help develop our "birthing plan."

Lord, help all of our plans to be made with the understanding that you remain as king over our lives.

Prayer (April 28)

"My brethren, count it all joy when you fall into various trials, knowing that the testing of your faith produces patience. But let patience have its perfect work, that you may be perfect and complete, lacking nothing. If any of you lacks wisdom, let him ask of God, who gives to all liberally and without reproach, and it will be given to him."
–James 1:2-5

For work, I started to support the "Go Live" of a new electronic medical record at a few hospitals about an hour away from home. This conveniently gave me an additional two hours each day to listen to some of the North American Week of Prayer recordings. Scott DeGroff shared some thoughts on hindrances to our prayer life and gave the following challenge, "Prayerlessness is a declaration of independence from God." As I texted a friend an update on how we were handling everything, I expressed that our prayers included us expressing our own personal desire for the miraculous healing of Jude, but our ultimate prayer was for God to work His perfect will in our lives and for us to trust Him through it.

Bike Rides & Rocks (April 30)

"In You, O Lord, I put my trust; let me never be ashamed; deliver me in Your righteousness. Bow down Your ear to me, deliver me speedily; be my rock of refuge, a fortress of defense to save me."
–Psalm 31:1-2

I felt the baby kick a few times last night. I was reminded of the extra challenges that Juli was facing. She was experiencing a much fuller demonstration of the life that was growing inside of her. I was continuing to gain a greater appreciation, respect, and understanding of the deep bond between mother and child and how this would make what we were going through that much more difficult for Juli.

We went to our kids' art show at their school, and I was able to see some of Juli's friends who had been especially comforting to her. I was sure to thank them as I knew how much Juli appreciated their hugs and words of comfort.

In considering the above verses, it's interesting that God brought me to a psalm that repeatedly reminded me of Him being my rock of refuge as we were outside of a restaurant and Dexter decided that today was the day to make the biggest rock collection he ever had. As he gathered the loose stones from the parking lot and shoved them in his pocket for safekeeping, I just chuckled. What is it with boys and their fascination with collecting rocks? Then, I considered the possibility of never being able to watch Jude collect rocks, but I was comforted knowing that he will be in the presence of the Rock of Refuge if he were to pass.

These thoughts often cross my mind as we join in on family activities. We went on a bike ride and I, being the over-achieving father and wonderful husband that I am, decided that I needed to put two kid seats on my bike so that my wife did not have the burden of carrying any of our children around (also due to the fact that Juli has an annual tradition of falling off of her bike at least once per year even without a baby in tow). Since Dexter started riding his own bike, I just had August in the seat behind me. During the entire ride, I rode through the streets of our neighborhood with an empty baby seat in between my handlebars...a constant reminder of the son who may never be able to fill that seat. I'm busy trying to hold back the tears and August is cracking up behind me having the time of his life. I love family bike rides!

Mother's Day (May 8)

"As one whom his mother comforts, so I will comfort you."
–Isaiah 66:13a

What an incredible thought that the most appropriate and fitting way that God can describe His love and care for His people is by comparing it to the comfort of a mother. But while the mother comforts the child, who comforts the mother. Well, the Lord does. I needed to be reminded to continually check in on Juli.

In the week leading up to Mother's Day, I knew that this was going to be a difficult one for Juli, so we had the opportunity to sit and talk about the little (and big) things that make her sad. She referenced a five-leafed plant (don't ask me what kind of plant it is) in our room in which the one leaf had turned brown and died and she thought about our kids. Four healthy, growing, thriving children and one that was not supposed to survive. The kids made a shirt for Juli and drew some of her favorite things with markers all over the shirt. In the family portrait on the back of the shirt, I saw that they did not include Jude in the picture, which was fine, but I realized that this might be the only Mother's Day that Juli would get to spend with him.

She also recalled getting an email about different available funeral homes following our meeting with the Pediatric Palliative Care team and shared that this email was just too much to process. A text from my friend, Ryan, guided us to trust in the Lord and to know that it's OK to not be OK as we grappled with the overwhelming emotions.

David pleads with God in Psalm 35:3b, "Say to my soul, 'I am your salvation.'" David is asking God to remind him of what he already knows. This is my prayer.

God, remind me of what I already know. You are my salvation!

Mother's Day Social Media Post (May 9)

Happy Mother's Day to all of the incredible moms out there. And especially to my wife! Thankful for your sacrificial love and godly example to our kids.

Juli and I were excited to find out this past winter that we were expecting baby #5. However, four months into the pregnancy, an ultrasound revealed that our son had a rare defect where he does not have any kidneys. Prognosis is not good, and we were told there is no chance of survival after delivery. We know God can work miracles, but we also continue to trust in the Lord in our current situation as we know His Plan and Purposes are Perfect.

Thank you for your prayers and may we all continue to appreciate and cherish every moment we have with the mothers in our lives. To the moms who are grieving, struggling, going through a difficult time. I pray that the below verses can provide strength and encouragement to press on in the incredible work you are doing.

"Whom have I in heaven but You? And there is none upon earth that I desire besides You. My flesh and my heart fail; But God is the strength of my heart and my portion forever. But it is good for me to draw near to God; I have put my trust in the Lord God, That I may declare all Your works."
–Psalm 73:25-26, 28

Shipwreck (May 11)

"When Paul saw them, he thanked God and took courage."
–Acts 28:15

In reading David Gooding's *True to the Faith*, Paul continued to have faith through the literal storms of his life. After recently suffering a violent shipwreck in the midst of a severe tempest at the island of Malta, Paul continued on to Rome and was encouraged simply by the sight of his brothers in the Lord. In the midst of this storm, Juli and I have often been encouraged by the comfort of knowing our brothers and sisters are right there beside us.

Memories That Will Never Be (May 13)

"Though He slay me, yet I will trust Him."
–Job 13:15

As I was reading Angie Smith's book, I was reminded that everyone grieves differently. My sister called Juli to vent about some seemingly trivial issue. While Juli listened, it was tough as she wished that the issue she was hearing over the phone was her own biggest problem right now. Angie Smith shared a letter that she wrote to her daughter who received the same diagnosis as Jude. It was sad thinking of all of the memories that would never happen as I reflected on our own story:

We already started to convert our garage into a new bedroom so you and your brothers could have a huge room to share and play in.
You were going to sleep on the bottom bunk, but eventually move to the top as you got older.
We were going to watch basketball games on TV together.

Despite the tendency to think that God was against me, I need to follow the example of Job and trust in God and trust that He knows what is best. I am slowly learning to trust that He has a reason and a plan for our family.

"Estrella" by Brave Saint Saturn

And isn't it just like me to mourn his passing breath
When he will never suffer anymore.
The angels' wings will cover you tonight, Hallelujah.
Press your head against the breast of Christ, Hallelujah.

Peace (May 18)

I started sharing our news with coworkers and found incredible support from Michael. As he shared his sympathy, he offered to help in any way possible. I shared about the comfort and strength that we find in our God and that it's only by His grace that we can have this peace that passes understanding.

One More, One Less (May 19)

Ultrasound appointments were much different compared to the other pregnancies. It felt like we were meeting up with a loved one that we didn't often get to see. We cherished these appointments as we felt as if we were experiencing Jude's presence in a more real way. Each ultrasound was more difficult as each additional visit meant one less appointment to look forward to. Normally, we wanted these appointments to end quickly, but now I'm secretly praying that they keep going. Seeing legs move, heart beating, lungs breathing. I felt like I was sneaking 100 photos of the ultrasound screen while getting dirty looks from the ultrasound technician.

This morning, I read Psalm 44:8, "In God we boast all day long and praise Your name forever." Then, our friend Scott shared it at prayer meeting (God hitting me with the same message from His Word both morning and night!). We then looked at Deuteronomy 8:1-4 where God tested the nation of Israel to see what was in their hearts. Through these trials, may we be found "strong in the grace that is in Christ Jesus" (2 Timothy 2:1).

I spoke with the Sharing Network (NJ organ donation organization) and asked about the possibility of Jude being an organ donor if he did not survive. We were told that he might not be eligible as a donor, but that a call would be made at the time of his passing to see if he could be a potential tissue donor. Thinking that if he passed, it would be such a blessing for another family to be helped by his brief life.

Built Different (May 20)

As I walked past our bathroom, I caught a glimpse of my wife in the most beautiful scene. There she was, glamorously standing at the bathroom sink, draped head-to-toe in her adult onesie while brushing her teeth, globs of toothpaste dripping down to the sink. Baby Jude was just chilling in her tummy, hanging out over the sink and I thought to myself...what a strong woman...she's built different.

While lying in bed later that night, Juli fell asleep, and I found a spot where Jude was punching (or kicking) and I just held my hand there as long as I could feel him. This was my father/son bonding time, just me and Jude. Perhaps the only "high fives" we might ever share, but how much I long to hold his hand when he is born.

How Long, O Lord? (May 24)

"How long, O Lord? Will You forget me forever?
How long will You hide Your face from me?
How long must I take counsel in my soul and have sorrow in my heart all day?"
—Psalm 13:1-2

"But I have trusted in Your steadfast love;
My heart shall rejoice in your salvation.
I will sing to the Lord, because He has dealt bountifully with me."
—Psalm 13:5-6

Our friend, Andrea, who had recently lost a son posted some thoughts on what one author considered David's darkest hour as expressed in Psalm 13. I read these verses as a prayer to God, honestly sharing how I felt, but trying my best to come to the same conclusion that David did. My coworker, Rob, who was aware of our son's diagnosis had reached out at the end of the workday and his thoughts touched me in a deep way. He and his wife were expecting a baby and out of courtesy and consideration for our situation wanted to check to see if it was ok for him to share his exciting news about his growing family. I was humbled by his sensitivity towards our family's situation, but honestly shared with him that our current circumstances gave us a greater appreciation for healthy pregnancies. While difficult at times to see others celebrating their healthy children, I knew that I was to rejoice with those who rejoice and weep with those who weep (Romans 12:15). Jude's diagnosis gave us a deeper passion for praying for others that were pregnant along with Juli.

We also received a package from Joan's Reach (an organization that provides support to families with difficult prenatal diagnoses). We were comforted by the books and resources that were gifted to us and read through a number of the books that were written to help kids understand and grasp the reality of the difficult news. Maggie had a softball game, but we skipped it to attend a ceremony for an award she had earned at school. Maggie and I decided to walk home, and we were able to talk about a variety of things, including how she felt about Jude's situation. She said she was sad, and I shared that I was sad, too. I reminded her (and probably just as much was reminding myself) that our family needed to choose to trust in God's perfect plan and to cherish whatever amount of time that we were granted to spend with Jude.

Those Who Rejoice (May 25)

I met baby Luke today. I could not help but rejoice with those who rejoice. Ryan and Nicole have been in deep prayer for us in our situation. I was so glad to share in the joy with this family who have been on a long journey themselves. Holding him obviously made me think of Jude afterwards, but in the moment, I could think of nothing except overwhelming happiness for this couple.

Hope in Your Word (May 28)

We attended the wedding of our friend, Jeremy. We all had a blast and while we were super excited for this couple, my mind kept circling back to the fact that I may never get to attend Jude's wedding. I kept reminding myself that this was a day to celebrate Jeremy and Autumn and not focus on ourselves. I had the opportunity to share a Scripture reading at the ceremony. Throughout the day, I was reminded that God was "my hiding place and my shield. I hope in Your Word" (Psalm 119:114).

He Fought to Stay (June 1)

I'm continuing to spend time in the Psalms. As I took a shower tonight, my mind kept fast-forwarding to the delivery day. My vision: the kids were drawing pictures for baby Jude, and we were having a big dance party in the hospital room with a happy healthy baby. I started to weep in the shower as I listened to a song that had been stuck in my head, one that I've considered time and time again after Jude's diagnosis:

"Estrella" by Brave Saint Saturn

And he fought to stay, but always dreamed that he could leave this place.
The angels' wings will cover you tonight, Hallelujah
Press your head against the breast of Christ, Hallelujah.

Severely Pained (June 2)

"You number my wanderings; Put my tears into Your bottle; Are they not in Your book?"
–Psalm 62:8

I was thinking of my tears last night. God knew they would be shed. It was recorded in His plan, and He was standing by, ready to collect them. He has already mapped (in detail) the journey that feels like an aimless wandering in a wilderness. We rest in His sovereignty. He sees the journey. He sees the end. I cry out:

"Be merciful to me, O God, be merciful to me!
For my soul trusts in You;
And in the shadow of Your wings, I will make refuge,
Until these calamities have passed by."
–Psalm 57:1

When David was running for his life, he reminded himself to wait patiently despite his tendency to wait anxiously.

Lord, help me to wait patiently. Remove my anxiety. Knowing the likely end has been burdensome to me, but my soul trusts in You. I take refuge in the shadow of Your wings.

Part of me wants to be on the other end of this year, but the other part of me wants to cherish what little time we have with Jude, wanting to savor every minute. As Juli and I sat on the couch, we were feeling non-stop punches and kicks. When people don't consider a fetus that is still in the womb a baby simply because he has not been delivered yet, my mind is just completely baffled. This is the only time that I will get to interact with my son. Don't tell me he's not alive.

"My heart is severely pained within me,
And the terrors of death have fallen upon me.
Fearfulness and trembling have come upon me,
And horror has overwhelmed me.
So, I said, 'Oh, that I had wings like a dove!
I would fly away and be at rest.
Indeed, I would wander far off,
And remain in the wilderness.' Selah
I would hasten my escape from the windy storm and tempest."
–Psalm 55:4-8

Look at the response…

"As for me, I will call upon God,
And the Lord shall save me.
Evening and morning and at noon
I will pray, and cry aloud,
And He shall hear my voice.
He has redeemed my soul in peace from the battle that was against me,
For there were many against me."
–Psalm 55:16-18

My niece, Madison, was born yesterday. We have been praying for the family and are super thrilled, but it was hard for Juli as she was part of a group chat with friends and some started to ask, "How was the first night with the baby?" These were normal questions following the birth of a baby and Juli knew that these conversations would be expected, but it was still hard for her to hear. I laid next to Juli on the couch and hugged her while feeling Jude still kick furiously. We were both crying, but we knew that God would take care us.

Mothers (June 7)

I was thinking of the narrative in Exodus and how Jochebed had to give up Moses after having him for three months simply to save his life from Pharaoh's law. I can't imagine the emotional toll that this would have taken on her. Hannah was another mom who "gave up" her son as she prayed for a child, she asked, "O Lord of hosts, if You will indeed look on the affliction of Your maidservant and remember me, and not forget Your maidservant, but will give Your maidservant a male child, then I will give him to the Lord all the days of his life" (1 Samuel 1:11).

Hannah was ready and willing to give her son (whom she recognized as a gift to her from God) back to the Lord for spiritual service. Are we willing to give our son back to the Lord, recognizing that he is a gift from God for whatever time we have with him?

"'Therefore, I also have lent him to the Lord; as long as he lives, he shall be lent to the Lord.' So, they worshiped the Lord there."
–1 Samuel 1:28

Lord, please look on our affliction and grant us the same spirit of Hannah. We ask for hearts that are ready and willing to give our son back to You. May our lending back to you lead us to worship You for Your goodness to us.

Each of these mothers had some sort of ongoing relationship with their son, but Moses' mother did not know that God would orchestrate an ongoing connection. Perhaps it is difficult for us as we won't see Jude if he passes, but we can still lend him to the Lord as long as he lives.

Baby Jude (June 9)

So, Augie's comprehension of our family situation with Jude is most likely more on his mind than we realize. He reminded me of my need to get back in shape as he stared at me with the cutest confused look I had ever seen. He kept looking at my belly, then back at my face, then back at my belly. With puzzled curiosity, he pointed at my belly and asked…

"Baby Jude?"

I told him "No" and that daddy just needed to stop eating so much ice cream. Kids are the best, aren't they?

Just Sad (June 10)

As we met with the wonderful Pediatric Palliative Care team at Monmouth Medical Center again, they helped us come up with a birth plan. This plan included what to expect leading up to delivery, at the time of delivery, and planning for after the birth. Part of this plan was a list of funeral homes. When we got home, Maggie asked Juli why they were giving us names of funeral homes. Juli explained again to the kids what was *expected* to happen from a medical perspective, reminding them that we can and should still pray for a miracle. Juli asked Maggie if she was still confused to which she replied, "No, I'm just sad."

Praise (June 11)

"Praise is awaiting You, O God, in Zion;
And to You the vow shall be performed.
O You who hear prayer,
To You all flesh will come."
–Psalm 65:1-2

I can't remember when we had decided on the name Jude, but his name means "Praised." I couldn't help but think of this verse as a reminder that Jude was "awaiting" God. While we waited for God, Jude was perhaps waiting to be in His presence.

"Blessed is the man You choose,
And cause to approach You,
That he may dwell in Your courts."
–Psalm 65:4

Jude may be dwelling in God's court long before us.

"By awesome deeds in righteousness You will answer us, O God of our salvation."
–Psalm 65:5

From Fire to Fulfillment (June 13)

"You have caused men to ride over our heads;
We went through fire and through water;
But You brought us out to rich fulfillment."
–Psalm 66:12

Juli and I watched an Amazon Prime series called *Night Sky* tonight. The show was about a family who stumbles upon a young man named Jude. The story describes a family's long-term grieving of a son they had lost in his 30s. I am sure this will be a lifelong journey, but how long is it going to be this difficult? I know it has been harder for Juli and I am sure it's largely in part to the fact that she is carrying our son. Will it be harder for me or for Juli? Will it hit us at different times and in different ways, triggered by different memories?

I was reading Psalm 66, and I am not much of a poet or songwriter, but the words of this Psalm brought me to write the below thoughts:

The net, the burden, the water and fire
These will bring forth what you so desire
Which of these, Lord, have You pulled me thru?
Nevertheless, it's all about You.

What about me? Am I all about You?
Are the prayers that I've cried, What You wanted me to?
All of the earth will sing Praise, Praise!
(I'll do the same) I Sing Praises to Your Name!

Awesome, and powerful, great to be praised
The works of Your hand are the reason we raise
A shout to Your victory, through seeming defeat
Hearts filled with sorrow, Rejoice, bowed at Your feet.

Wounded and beaten, defeated and broken
To You I have cried, to You I have spoken,
And You've heard my cry, You've spoken to me
Whom the Son shall set free, shall be free indeed!

Come & See (the works of our God)
Come & See (awesome in Power)
Come & See (done towards the children of men)

Come & Hear (All you who fear God)
Come & Hear (And I will declare what...)
Come & Hear (what He has done for my soul)

My friend Todd recommended a book by Nancy Pearcey (2018) entitled *Love Thy Body*. It had a strange title but a very timely book when attempting to address some of the cultural trends that we see in society today from a Christian worldview. In dealing with the sanctity of life, she writes:

"In the United States, many laws against abortion were passed in the nineteenth century, when medical knowledge first established that life begins at conception. That's when the genetic die is cast. On purely scientific grounds, older concepts were ruled irrelevant, such as quickening (the moment when a mother starts to feel the baby moving) or the moment when the baby takes its first breath. As a result, it was physicians – not churches – who were the legal advocates for laws criminalizing abortion.

Of course, people are much more than biological organisms and biology is not the most important dimension to life. Yet biology gives a baseline for identifying who is human. It is an objective, empirically testable, universally detectable marker of human status. The body is something that we can see and identify scientifically – something we can all agree on. Human beings reproduce 'after their kind,' just as Genesis 1 says. Thus, everyone who is human is also a person; they do not need to meet any additional criteria.

By contrast, personhood theory says some humans do not qualify as persons. In that case, how do we determine which humans *do* qualify? How do we identify the additional criteria they must meet? As we have seen, no two bioethicists agree on what personhood is or when it begins. Their definitions are purely subjective, reflecting their own personal values."

For us, we recognized the reality of Jude as a human, as a *person* in the womb. This perspective directly contradicts the post-modern worldview that clings to the personhood theory with no consistent objective definition of what makes a human a person. Please don't tell me my son has not qualified as a person yet.

Jude Tree (June 14)

I'm not much of an arborist, but we planted a few trees on our property to replace the dead and ugly ones that we got rid of. The tree directly in front of our front door is a tri-color beech. We have labeled this one as the "Jude Tree." It was emotional watching Augie carry a watering can that was even bigger than him and water this tree. Just read these verses this morning.

"Blessed be the Lord,
Who daily loads us with benefits,
The God of our salvation! Selah
Our God is the God of salvation;
And to God the Lord belong escapes from death."
–Psalm 68:19-20

"Draw near to my soul, and redeem it;
Deliver me because of my enemies.
You know my reproach, my shame, and my dishonor;
My adversaries are all before You.
Reproach has broken my heart,
And I am full of heaviness;
I looked for someone to take pity, but there was none;
And for comforters, but I found none."
–Psalm 69:18-20

Lord, we look for comfort in You, in the midst of our heaviness and broken hearts. May we be reminded of the daily benefits that You load on us. Draw near to our souls.

Needy (June 15)

"Let all those who seek You rejoice and be glad in You;
And let those who love Your salvation say continually,
'Let God be magnified!'
But I am poor and needy;
Make haste to me, O God!
You are my help and my deliverer;
O LORD, do not delay."
–Psalm 70:4-5

Lord, teach me to love Your salvation more and more. No matter the circumstances, let me say continually, "Let God be magnified!"

Tiles & Tombstones (June 17)

So, I thought I would be the only one to completely evade it, but seven months after the rest of the family had come down with COVID, I finally got it. I just finished three shifts in a row supporting the new Epic Go Live at RWJ New Brunswick and, of course, most of my shift was spent on their COVID unit. After those three shifts, we brought the family to our local theme park, Six Flags Great Adventure, so I thought I was just overheated and over-exhausted, but I simply could not get out of bed the next morning. After isolating in the basement for two days, I felt almost fully recovered.

Juli started having Braxton-Hicks contractions which was a little bit of a wake-up call, reminding us that Jude's arrival might be just around the corner. The renovations on our garage conversion were coming along. Privately to myself, I referred to this new room as the Jude Room, since although it was planned to be our new master bedroom/bathroom, we were getting the update due to our growing family. I was finally fulfilling the promise I made to Juli 10 years ago that one day she would get the master bedroom/bathroom combo that she deserved (took me long enough). Our renovation guy, Baker, needed us to pick out some tile for the new shower.

I brought Dexter on a ride with me to the tile store. After picking out some tile and supplies, we stopped by the Woodbine Cemetery to check out some options for burial plots and services. This was where my dad's parents were buried along with many of his aunts and uncles. This was also where my parents have reservations (kind of like dinner reservations, but not as fun). I thought that if we were to pick a spot for Jude's body, it would be nice to have the family all in one place.

This felt strange. As we were just looking for building materials for the room that we were creating to make more space for Jude, we were now looking to purchase a space for him at the cemetery. I had some really good conversations with Dexter as he was quite curious about the concept of a body being buried. I reminded him that if Jude passes, this was just going to be a resting place for his body even though he would be in heaven. He still had tons of questions (which often consisted of just asking "Why?" after everything I said).

I read an article on www.desiringgod.org in which the author brought the reader to Psalm 119:75:

"I know, O Lord, that Your judgments are right,
And that in faithfulness You have afflicted me."

How can what God be doing in our life right now be *right*? How is He revealing

His faithfulness in His affliction toward me? The author posed this question: "What kind of loving father intentionally gives his child pain when he asks for joy? Our Heavenly Father often lets us wrestle with that question for some time, allowing the pain to do its sanctifying work."

Your Words Were Heard (June 18)

I was encouraged by something I read in Daniel 10:12 where Daniel is told, "Do not fear, Daniel, for from the first day that you set your heart to understand, and to humble yourself before your God, your words were heard; and I have come because of your words." I feel like we are in the middle of this process of setting our hearts to understand, but what a great reminder.

Lord, do You hear my words and hear my cry? Help me to understand. Teach me to humble myself before You so You will hear me and come to me because of my words like Daniel.

Conversations with Strangers (June 21)

We went to one of our favorite breakfast joints, MeeMom's, for breakfast with our friends, Teresa, Christine, and Deanna. The last time we were here was the day before we found out about Jude's diagnosis. We know that so many places and things will continue to trigger memories of Jude which we know will make the upcoming months (and perhaps years) more difficult. As we were walking out from our delicious, sugar-filled French toast breakfast, a mom and her daughter stopped Juli. They were asking her about the baby and the daughter was so excited for the baby that she started rubbing Juli's belly. Deanna commented to me that it must be very difficult at times for Juli as she has had many conversations with people who ask about the pregnancy. I agreed and shared that she handles each interaction differently.

I don't often find myself in these conversations with strangers as most are not aware of what's going on, but Juli doesn't really have the option of hiding it. Unfortunately, she finds herself needing to share perhaps at times when it is emotionally too difficult to talk about. If it's a brief conversation, she typically will just tell them the due date and the fact that it's a boy. However, as people continue to ask questions in their joy and excitement for the new baby, she would sometimes try to share briefly about the prognosis. Juli handled it with such a spirit of grace, reminding people that there is no need to apologize for asking. Her strength amazes me, and it is truly incredible to see her share the faith that she has in the God who continues to give her strength for each day.

It's also wonderful to see how strangers display a certain amount of love for our son already. He is loved even before his official grand entry into this world.

Faith like a Child (June 23)

I attended a virtual monthly missionary prayer meeting, and two missionaries were sharing about their trips to war-torn countries where they would see such devastating occurrences such as families' homes going up in smoke or fathers who were killed in war. A reminder that we are not the only ones going through hard times and heartache. In fact, life isn't so bad when compared to the tragedies that we hear about across the globe. My niece Madison was just admitted to the hospital with RSV, and it served as a reminder to pray for others even in our darkest times. Sometimes, in those dark times, we get so focused on ourselves that we can't see anyone else. We're reminded to pray for all men (1 Timothy 2:1).

Not even sure if I shared this yet because Augie has done it multiple times, but once again as we prayed for baby Jude and said "Amen," Augie started yelling, "No! No! We pray for a miracle!"

Lord, give me faith like a child.

Heartbeat (June 25)

"Will the Lord cast off forever?
And will He be favorable no more?
Has His mercy ceased forever?
Has His promise failed forevermore?
Has God forgotten to be gracious?
Has He in anger shut up His tender mercies?"
–Psalm 77:7-9

Some of the same doubts and questions come to my mind as I read the words of Asaph, but we think back to God's faithfulness throughout all of August's ordeal. God did not forget us then and He will not forget us now. God's promises didn't fail then, and they won't fail now. As I listened to Dr. Dave Reid's outline of Psalm 77 (www.growingchristians.org), I appreciated how he divided the above psalm into two parts:

1. Verses 1-9: "Doubt Arises during Times of Distress and Despair"
2. Verses 10-20: "Reassurance Arises during Times of Remembrance"

We must remember the works and the wonders of our God (verses 11 and 14). He will continue to strengthen and lead us (verses 14 and 20) as He always does. We listened to Jude's heartbeat with the doppler again. We recorded the kids and their joyful reaction and excitement to hearing their baby brother's heartbeat. Dexter and Augie listened intently and carefully to make sure they could hear. Due to the low amniotic fluid, the sound was not the strongest and so when we lost the heartbeat for a brief moment, Dexter asked, "Is he dead?" We very quickly picked up the heartbeat again and Dexter sighed a sigh of relief. As we put the doppler to Augie's chest, he exclaimed, "I hear him!" No, Augie…that's your heart.

I spoke with my sister about some of the logistical things like looking for a cemetery plot and preparing for the birth and the funeral at the same time (despite our prayer for a miracle, the Pediatric Palliative Care team at MMC was very wise to guide us to make preparations so as to not be unprepared). I think I've gotten it down to a science, the ability to shut my emotions down in order to function at work. I'm still trying to trust God through it all.

Rock & Redeemer (June 28)

The difficulties in life often cause us to return and seek the Lord after a season of wandering. We forget Him. We get entangled with the cares of this world. We suffer, but then our trials remind us that He is our Rock and our Redeemer.

"When He slew them, then they sought Him;
And they returned and sought earnestly for God.
Then they remembered that God was their Rock,
And the Most High God their Redeemer."
–Psalm 78:34-35

Does the Lord need to slay me in order for me to seek Him?

Lord, help me to seek You in the good times and the bad times, through stormy seas and through smooth sailing. Remind me of the solid Rock upon which I stand and the price that was paid for my redemption.

For the Glory of Your Name (June 29)

My nephew, Jackson, keeps telling my sister that he doesn't want Aunt Juli's baby to die. Through his tears, he was hugging Juli's belly over and over again. I've really learned to appreciate having family around and having family that loves us through all of life's battles. August, Juli, and I got to hold Madison for the very first time today and it was difficult as we held that precious little girl thinking of how we may have very limited time to hold our son. Augie yelled out, "Mommy, baby Madison is so cute!"

I've been reading *God of the Garden* by Andrew Peterson and he describes a story in which a boy suffers the devastating loss of a deer that he befriended.

"After the worst happens, the little boy's world is wrecked, and he realizes that grief and sorrow are humankind's inescapable lot. The sorrow is unstoppable. Doom is imminent. I have tried to protect my children, however falteringly, from the grief that hovers on the horizon of their lives like a gathering storm. But there's nothing for it. They're going to wound and get wounded. Seeing your children's innocence fray can remind you of the shredded grave cloth of your own, and memories long buried claw their way out of the earth to demand answers" (Peterson, 2021, pp. 97-98).

I really wonder what it's going to look like as we try to help carry our kids through the grief. Hopefully they can look at Juli and I and see us trusting in God to carry us through our own sorrow.

"Oh, do not remember former iniquities against us!
Let Your tender mercies come speedily to meet us,
For we have been brought very low.
Help us, O God of our salvation,
For the glory of Your name;
And deliver us, and provide atonement for our sins,
For Your name's sake!"
–Psalm 79:8-9

We often ask for help from God for our life to be improved (easier, more comfortable, more satisfying), but verse 9 reminds us that our goal in asking for help should be for the glory of His name!

In praying for a miracle, we are essentially asking God for help. Is it a selfish thing to ask for a healthy baby? Wouldn't God's name receive the most glory if He gave us a miracle? If not, we need to ask how we can practically display the goodness and greatness of God in our situation, no matter the outcome. Is experiencing the end of verse 8 ("being brought very low") also "for the glory of His name" (verse 9)?

Nate Bramsen's *Into Your Bible* series through Exodus continues to get me thinking as he shared these reflections:

"If you want to know God as your Comforter, do you expect Him to zap you with the mere knowledge *or* provide you the experience where you will taste His comfort?

"To know Him as Comforter, there is a prerequisite of grief or distress.
To know God as your Healer, there is a prerequisite of sickness or disease.
To know God as your Strength, there is a prerequisite of weakness. In that His strength is made perfect.

To know God as your Provider, there is a prerequisite of need.
To know God as your Peace, there is a prerequisite of unrest.
To know God as your Sustainer, there is a prerequisite of a prolonged trial.
To know God as your Defender, there is a prerequisite of being accused.
To know God as your Resurrection, there is a prerequisite of the grave."

A missionary visited our chapel tonight and shared a similar sentiment while bringing us through Luke 4. The moments that Jesus gives us in the wilderness are for a purpose. Ultimately, it is to provide us with an opportunity to learn to trust and lean on Him.

A Little More Personal – Social Media Post (June 29)

As Juli and I discussed some of the below thoughts with each other, we firmly believe that our personal decisions and convictions are based on a biblical worldview. Historically, the US has been considered a "Christian" nation. We understand that this has shifted over the years and that many people may hold vastly different worldviews or come to very different conclusions, but we share the below thoughts jointly knowing that all people in this world are hurting and all of humanity is in desperate need of redemption, forgiveness and love that can only be found in Jesus Christ. By the grace of God, may we all strive to do our best to love one another, despite our differences:

When Juli and I found out that our baby had no kidneys and was medically not going to survive long after birth, we were presented with three options: (1) an "experimental" clinical trial with uncertain outcomes (2) "interrupting" the pregnancy (3) carrying the baby to term while knowing the expected outcome.

Personally, for us, #2 was not an option and after much thought and prayer, we decided on option #3. Following the diagnosis, as the weeks turned into months, we began to grasp the reality of what we expected, that this would be a more difficult road (physically, emotionally, and financially). All the while (and still) praying for a miracle, we both realized that the only time we may get to spend with our son would be in the womb. We have never cherished any other pregnancy as much as this one.

Through each of our pregnancies, we cannot help but love the little life that is growing inside the womb and mourn for the potential loss of life we may soon experience.

Each night, we watch and feel the little kicks and punches, knowing that this might be the only chance we get. When the kids lay their hands on Juli's belly, they are thrilled to feel their sibling literally reaching out. When they come up to Juli and kiss her belly, their hearts are pouring over with love for a sibling that they look forward to meeting soon. Our hearts are filled with joy as Dexter jumps with excitement after hugging Juli and getting kicked in the face by his unborn little bro.

…Unsettled Reflection…

As I considered the recent Supreme Court decision, my mind went back to an earlier time in my marriage when my wife and I were faced with joy, sorrow, and confusion all at the same time. I share the below story in hopes that we all would gain a divine perspective when faced with difficult decisions, even as I frequently, yet hesitantly, revisit this part of my life often in my own mind…

In 2012, we found out that Juli was pregnant, and we were thrilled with the news and excited to share with our family. On a trip down to Florida, just before we were planning on sharing the news, Juli noticed some bleeding. Our joy quickly turned into concern as were not sure now how to share the news with our family. What we were expecting to be an exciting announcement became a worry-filled conversation. As Juli talked to her mom, she shared that we were expecting, but that she noticed some bleeding and wanted to get checked out to see if everything was OK.

Since we were out-of-town, we decided to go to the local Emergency Department. After checking us in and getting us registered, they took some blood work and performed an ultrasound. At first, they were suggesting that Juli might be having a miscarriage, but imaging suggested that she was experiencing an ectopic pregnancy. Without getting into too much detail, the typical implantation of an ectopic pregnancy was somewhere in the fallopian tubes, but this was in the cervix, a very rare location for this to occur. Either way, this was now a potentially life-threatening situation for Juli. If the baby continued to develop in the cervix, this would ultimately result in the death of the baby and severe hemorrhaging for Juli. Perhaps in my desperate search for hope or my lack of paying attention in nursing school (or a combination of both), I asked if there was any way to move and re-implant the baby into the correct location in the uterus. We felt hopeless, but at the same time hoping the initial diagnosis was wrong. They asked us to come back to the ED to check Juli's HCG levels, so we returned back to my in-laws with perhaps more questions than answers.

We returned to the Emergency Department two days later to recheck the HCG levels and do a repeat ultrasound to confirm the findings. Following the bloodwork, one of the ED physicians came into our room and said, "Congratulations, you're still pregnant!" He was under the impression that the conclusion from the last visit was a miscarriage was taking place (HCG levels remained high, whereas in a miscarriage the level would have dropped significantly). We were even more thoroughly confused as we were expecting confirmation of the cervical ectopic pregnancy, but now we thought that there was a misdiagnosis from last visit. A glimmer of hope, perhaps?

This interaction was quite bewildering as our sorrow turned to joy, thinking the baby was in a viable place to develop. However, upon addressing our concern with the physician, he left the room to review the chart and realized his mistake that indeed the HCG levels would continue to remain high (*not* a miscarriage), but that the baby could not continue to grow in his or her current physical location.

And now the heartbreaking reality. Despite repeated questioning of what possible ways we could intervene to save this child's life, the message was reinforced with us over and over. There was no way that this child could fully develop and survive and if permitted to grow, Juli would hemorrhage and be in a life-threatening situation. So, we were faced with a choice (if we can call it that):

Option 1: Allow our child to develop and put Juli's life at risk of bleeding out as the baby grew in size.

OR

Option 2: "Interrupt" the growth of the baby to save Juli's life.

If you were to ask us on any given day our thoughts on abortion, both Juli and I would unashamedly and assuredly affirm that neither of us support the ending of a child's life in the womb. But now we came face-to-face with a dreaded reality. Medically speaking, there was absolutely no chance that this child could fully develop and survive, but if left to develop, Juli's life would be at significant risk of being lost.

What should we choose? What was the right option morally? Would God ever approve of a situation where we choose to end the life of a child in the womb? In reading Nancy Pearcey's *Love Thy Body*, this argument of the biological *life* in the womb not yet becoming a *person* embraces the secular worldview of dualism, which creates this imaginary line and man-made distinction between the two, a distinction that the Word of God never makes. We fully believe that a child in the womb is a unique life for a variety of reasons. This is perhaps not the time and place to dig deep into the philosophical, biological, and legal reasons why I believe this, let alone the biblical reasons, but I refer you to a message I shared at our church regarding God's perspective on the sanctity of human life (see Resources & References at the end of the book).

Scripture makes it clear that God alone has the power and authority to put to death and bring to life (Deuteronomy 32:39; 1 Samuel 2:6) and in fact, He does not take pleasure in the death of the wicked (Ezekiel 33:11), let alone the putting to death of an innocent life in the womb. I will often revisit the decision we made and ask myself if we were justified in the choice that we made. A conversation with my good friend Timm reiterated the truth and reality that is found throughout the pages of Scripture (as referenced above):

God.
Values.
Life.

In choosing between the loss of my wife *and* our child versus the loss of our child, after much thought and prayer, we felt a peace in deciding to value life from what we believe was God's perspective. Was this not the same as an abortion? Were we justified in our actions? Juli ended up receiving the series of methotrexate injections to end our child's life. Despite the belief that we made the choice that would preserve as much life as possible, there remains this unsettled feeling every time that I think back to this day.

The healthcare team gave us instructions on when it was safe to fly back to NJ, but the turmoil within my own heart grew even greater as we returned home and had a follow-up appointment with Juli's doctor. Upon follow-up ultrasound after the methotrexate series, the technician could hear a strong heartbeat. It was as if our baby was still fighting for his/her life despite our evil and cruel attempts to end it. We were torn apart on the inside and despite our resolve that we made the right decision, we could not help but be gripped by the guilt of the choice that we made. Our kid was a fighter.

Our hearts were broken as this was our first pregnancy and it ended in such a devastating way. I will occasionally think back to 2012 and ask God for understanding and even forgiveness if a better choice could have been made. My prayer is also that by sharing our personal journey that each and every one of us would seek to do the will of our sovereign God as opposed to simply choosing to do what is most convenient for our own lives. May each of us grow in our comprehension of the will of God and thus make choices that align with the mind of God (Philippians 2:5).

Praying for Miracles (June 30)

"You called in trouble, and I delivered you;
I answered you in the secret place of thunder;
I tested you at the waters of Meribah."
–Psalm 81:7

We had our Bible Study that we do with some old friends from high school, and I know I have mentioned already how much of a blessing this group is to me. We were on the beach that night and I was reminded of how appreciative I am for friends who are willing to talk and support me in prayer. We sang the below song together:

"Yes I Will" by Vertical Worship

I count on one thing
The same God that never fails
Will not fail me now
You won't fail me now
In the waiting
The same God who's never late
Is working all things out
You're working all things out

Yes I will, lift You high in the lowest valley
Yes I will, bless Your name
Oh, yes I will, sing for joy when my heart is heavy
All my days, oh yes I will

My friend Ryan shared about a friend who was having difficulty getting pregnant. He shared how he and his wife had the opportunity to pray with her and now she is pregnant with triplets! I so appreciate his prayers for our family as he is truly praying in faith for Jude to be healed. We talked about the balance I am trying to have (and struggling with), fully believing that God can heal, but understanding that a miracle may also not be a part of His will for Jude or for us.

Are we doubting? Won't God receive the most glory if Jude is miraculously healed AND this friend of Ryan and Nicole's has a healthy pregnancy and birth?

If, and I repeat *if*, God were to only intervene in one of these situations, wouldn't it be best for the divine intervention to be for the non-believer, that she would see the power of God and turn to Christ? If Jude passes, from the little that we read in Scripture, we believe he is in heaven! If their friend were to die without Christ, we know in Scripture she is headed for a lost eternity. We are praying for her salvation! God desires that all men should come to repentance and that none should perish (2 Peter 3:9).

Assumptions (July 1)

"I know, O Lord, that Your judgments are right,
And that in faithfulness You have afflicted me."
–Psalm 119:75

Maggie asked, "Daddy, does Aunt Kristin love Uncle Jimmy more than you?"
To which I replied, "Maggie...Why would you ask that?"
"Because she says she's going to Hershey Park with Uncle Jimmy, but she wouldn't go to Hurricane Harbor with you."

Kids don't always get it or understand the reasons why certain things happen. They often will see the end result and make judgments or assumptions while not fully knowing the details around specific circumstances. Do we make assumptions about God's love for us (or seemingly lack thereof) when things turn out a certain way?

Neighbors (July 2)

I was working up in New Brunswick, supporting the Go Live of the new electronic medical record. It was a beautiful evening, but 45 minutes south, a nasty storm was hitting our town with hail, wind, rain, and downed trees. Juli sent me a picture of our neighbor's tree that was torn apart during the storm. They were safe, but the tree hit their home and an electrical wire was down in the road blocking our road. On the drive into our neighborhood, my detour took me past the house of a classmate from high school. She was out in her front yard walking the dog. I asked her how her sister was doing (her sister, Abbey, was the one who had given us the doppler to hear Jude's heartbeat...we had been praying for Abbey and her son's health complications). She shared that they were waiting for the baby to grow until he was big enough to have the necessary surgery, but that he was stable. She asked how we were doing and shared some of her own personal losses that she had gone through. I knew God had directed me on this detour because I had such an incredibly encouraging conversation with her. She blessed me with the following reminders:

–*Don't be afraid to feel your emotions. It's not beneficial to suppress what you are feeling and try to just look on the bright side of things.*
–*Emotions will change from one minute to the next, so cry when you need to cry, hurt when you need to hurt, and have peace when you feel like having peace.*

I was reminded of the peace of God that we are promised, but I acknowledged to myself that at times we may not necessarily *feel* that peace. What a reminder to be honest with others about our emotions I am slowly learning that being honest with others helps us be honest with God.

The intensity and raw emotions of the writer of Psalm 80 are felt below as he cries out to God:

"O LORD God of hosts,
How long will You be angry
Against the prayer of Your people?
You have fed them with the bread of tears,
And given them tears to drink in great measure."
–Psalm 80:1-4

In *The God of the Garden*, Andrew Peterson explains that "we need stories. Stories need places. Places need people, and people need homes. We were made for community, but so many things about this in-between world of no-places seem designed to hinder it instead."

I appreciate living in my town. My neighbors are the best and so many friends from high school that we grew up still live here. Developing a strong sense of community has been quite easy when considering our incredible neighbors and family that surround us. I just went outside to hug Alisa (whose massive tree had just landed on her house) and talk to some other neighbors. We have a community here and I love it. Sometimes life is too busy to really spend time together, but it's comforting to know that they are there for us when we need them! Also, it helps knowing that every neighbor on our block has offered to let our kids use their pool (not that this is the only reason that we appreciate our neighbors so much, but it's a big perk).

THE BEGINNING OF AUGUST (JULY 4)

We had long been expecting the arrival of our baby boy at the beginning of August. His due date was actually the same day as our wedding anniversary. Jude had other plans…

I woke up on the morning of the Fourth of July and a bunch of the parents of my daughter's classmates got together to play soccer, so I joined them. I went home afterwards, did the dishes, loaded up some laundry, and sat down to watch a movie with the kids. I was working that night in New Brunswick, so I went to sleep around noon. I continued my typical routine prior to working the nightshift by picking up my sausage, egg, and cheese on a croissant along with my coffee from Dunkin'. When I arrived in the parking garage, I jumped out of my car in a hurry and grabbed the wrong ID badge (little did I know that this would make tonight a little more challenging).

After working a few hours, I began to get text messages from Juli who shared that she was feeling like she was getting those Braxton-Hicks contractions again, but this time she said it felt different. We talked for a bit, and I told Juli to keep an eye on the contractions and see if they got better or worse and to call the emergency number for her doctor if things went in that direction. She was nervous and started praying that God would delay Jude's arrival. A short while later, I got a text, and she told me that the doctor had told her to go to the hospital. I told my coworker that I had to go, but as I rushed to get my things together, I ran out of the office and finally realized that I had grabbed the wrong badge. As I went from the elevators to the main hospital, I realized that I would not be able to access the direct route through the hospital to get to where my car was parked. I was now trapped in an area where I couldn't get back into the office or walk through the main hospital. I frantically searched for a stairwell and sprinted down to the street level. I ran. New Brunswick is not the safest place to be running down the streets at 1 a.m., but my own personal safety was the last thing on my mind. Exhausted and out of breath, I finally got to my car. It would take me another 50 minutes to get to Monmouth Medical Center where Juli was delivering, and I was hoping and praying I would get there in time to meet Jude. I knew that we were told we may not have all that much time with him and I was determined to be there.

I raced down Route 18 as my brother Jim picked up Juli and brought her to the hospital. If I had not been pulled over for speeding on that same road two days earlier, I would have gone faster, but I tried to keep it to a steady 5mph over the speed limit. The last thing I needed was to be pulled over and miss Jude's birth for certain. While I was driving, Juli asked me to contact the photographer from Now I Lay Me Down to Sleep (an organization that offers photography sessions for situations like ours that we connected with through Joan's Reach). It was 1:30 a.m. She picked up and asked what time we wanted her there.

When I arrived at the hospital, Jim went back to our house to pick up our kids. Dr. Smith recommended what we had discussed regarding the plan for a C-section and that we would be heading back in about 30 minutes. This was going to be Juli's first C-section so that was weighing on her mind as far as not knowing what to expect. I did share with the staff my history of passing out during C-sections just so they could catch me in case they saw me going down. We had so many questions, though. What was the timeframe? What should we expect? What was Jude's assessment going to be like? How long would they take him for?

We couldn't believe the day that we were anticipating for so long was finally here. The day that we both dreaded and longed for at the same time. I think we were just so overwhelmed by all of the activity that we really didn't have much time to process what we were really feeling. I gowned up and the doctor asked Juli what music she wanted playing in the delivery room. She told her to ask me. I hadn't even thought about it, but my mind went straight to a lullaby album by JJ Heller that each of our kids loved to go to sleep to. They continued to set Juli up as I messaged updates to Juli's family from the other room.

They brought me back and it seemed like Jude arrived fairly quickly. There he was. I saw him and I crossed the hall as the nursing staff carried him over for a quick assessment. The first question in my mind was if he would miraculously have far more developed lungs than they expected. Would they be able to save him? He didn't seem like he was in distress and perhaps everything was going to be just fine. But as they assessed him, they told me that his HR was much lower than expected and I could see his breaths were much slower than I anticipated. They told me that he would not survive long. I wanted to get him back to Juli to allow her to spend whatever time we had with him together. As they stitched Juli up, she was trying to process the pain, the cold, the awkward feeling of organs shifting around inside her, but all went well as we held our precious boy, watching and cherishing every little breath that he took, every second that we had with him.

We took turns holding him, kissing him, holding his hand, caressing his face. By the time they brought us back to the room, I think his breaths had slowed so much and was not sure if he was even still with us. Jim had gotten our kids to the hospital and the photographer had arrived and began taking pictures. He was born at 2:57 a.m. and the doctors pronounced him at 4:16 a.m. He most likely passed before that, but I think the staff were trying to not interrupt our family time. Obviously, this was heartbreaking for the kids. It was heartbreaking for us, too. Maggie proudly held her baby brother as she gently rocked him.

Wesley held him and tenderly stroked his cheek. Dexter was asking a lot of pointed questions but was hesitant to hold and kiss Jude because I believe he was slowly realizing what was going on. August was hesitant at first, too. They were all realizing what was happening. The kids took turns holding him shortly after he died, and we shared with them that we had to say goodbye because he had gone to be with Jesus.

The photographer took some family photos, some close-ups and one with all of the kids together. We were so grateful as she stayed with us for almost two hours. We thanked her and asked her how she got connected with this organization. She told us that she had lost her own child suddenly following a healthy pregnancy and her photographer had left such a wonderful impression on her that she wanted to help others in the same way. We don't always realize how much pain the ones around us are going through.

The birthing plan we set up with Maria and Susan in our meetings was to let Jude's body go as soon as he died. We thought of the verse in Scripture that remind us "to be absent from the body is to be present with the Lord" (2 Corinthians 5:8). Even though I felt as if we were pretty set on this, we were so glad that they kept reminding us that we could change our birthing plan at any time. He was no longer with us, but we held on to him for a few reasons.

He died much sooner than we had anticipated, and we wanted more time…more time for photos…more time for my parents to come in and get a chance to meet their grandson. Juli and I also came to the realization that his body was the last physical, tangible memory that we would have of him. It was a lot tougher to let go than we had anticipated. I know that since my wife had a closer physical connection to our son that this process might be more difficult. I was reminded in Nancy Pearcey's *Love Thy Body* that the bodies that we have are a big part of who God uniquely created us to be. Even though Jude's spirit was gone, his body was a part of who he was and who God created him to be.

Juli and I wrestled within our minds of when to let him go. We took turns holding him, realizing that the entire night/day had been a whirlwind. We danced with him. We were falling asleep as we held him, trying to cherish every moment that we would have with him until we had no energy left to stay awake, both of us exhausted and sleep deprived. We let his body go some time after midnight that day. I write this with fresh tears in my eyes knowing that this was our final farewell to him.

We would never again get a chance to say goodnight.
A chance to change his diaper.
A chance to read him a bedtime story.
A chance for him to crawl into bed with us after having a scary dream.

A chance to take first and last day of school pictures.
A chance to cheer for him at his soccer or baseball games.
To drop him off at Greenwood Hills Boys' Camp.
To learn to ride a bike.
To teach him how to swim.
To celebrate birthdays.
To open Christmas presents.
To see him graduate, get married, have kids.

Jude Phineas Cagliostro
Social Media Post (July 5)

Jude Phineas Cagliostro arrived on 7/5/22 at 2:57 a.m., 6 lbs and 17 in. We had a precious 30 minutes with him before he went to be with our Lord and Savior. Juli and the kids are doing well, and we all got to spend some quality family time together. Please pray for peace and comfort as we rest in His promises.

The name "Jude" means "Praise" and even in this deepest of sorrows, we will praise our God!

How can someone praise God in such awful circumstances?

Psalm 34:1 declares, "His praise shall always be on my lips." There is a time to mourn and a time to laugh (Ecclesiastes 3:1-4), but we can continually praise Him through all of life's ups and downs.

In Scripture, when Daniel's friends refused to bow down to the king's golden image, they whole-heartedly believed that God could deliver them from the punishment of death that was pronounced on them. Their response...

"Shadrach, Meshach, and Abed-Nego answered and said to the king, 'O Nebuchadnezzar, we have no need to answer you in this matter. If that is the case, our God whom we serve is able to deliver us from the burning fiery furnace, and He will deliver us from your hand, O king. ***BUT IF NOT***, let it be known to you, O king, that we do not serve your gods, nor will we worship the gold image which you have set up.'"
–Daniel 3:16-18

...But if not...

Even if they were not delivered, they would continue to trust in their God...

...But if not...

With full assurance, we believed God could provide a miracle for Jude...

...But if not...

In conversations with our daughter as she questioned God's providence in the situation, we shared our personal belief that even if God doesn't answer our prayers the way that we want, it doesn't mean that He is not there. Despite the outcome, we firmly believe that God is sovereign, and we will continually praise Him. We truly miss our precious son, but we are incredibly grateful for how EVERYTHING worked out so perfectly...

Thank you to my brother Jim for getting Juli to the hospital while I was up in New Brunswick working the nightshift. And for coordinating getting our kids to the hospital to meet their baby brother.

Thank you to the incredible teams in L&D, NICU, and pediatric palliative care at Monmouth Medical Center! You truly know how to take a heart-wrenching situation and turn it into one filled with beautiful memories.

Thank you, Mom/Dad & Jim/Lisa, for watching our kids during Juli's recovery.

Thank you, Fifth Avenue Chapel family, for your continual outpouring of love, care, and compassion on our entire family.

Thank you to all of our family and friends for your constant prayer and support!

For now...we sorrow...but we also rejoice...as the Word of God reminds us that we do not need to sorrow as those who have no hope (1 Thess. 4:13). Our hope is in Christ who offers life and forgiveness to all who will repent and call on His name.

Peace...Comfort...Joy...Hope...

These are what we have found in our short time with Jude, and this is what can be found for all who seek and find Christ.

Stuck (July 5)

I keep reading Psalm 86 over and over again. This was the psalm that I was in the process of reading ever since I began reading through the Psalms on this journey with Jude. I feel like I'm stuck on it, like the Lord is trying to speak to me through it, or perhaps it's as if I can't move on from this chapter because of its timing in relation to Jude's birth, but what a powerful psalm. Go read it.

Flowers & Friends (July 6)

We started working on funeral arrangements and decided on cremation. This would give us more time to prepare, more time for Juli to heal physically, more time to allow Juli's family to make plans to travel up here for a memorial service…and let's be honest…it was much cheaper. I spoke with the funeral home director who was actually a former student of my mom. This funeral home was recommended by Susan from MMC, and she had contacted them ahead of time on our behalf. All of our immediate family members were aware of all that transpired as many of them were on the phone with us throughout the day. We started to share updates with extended family and friends. I sent a group text to my Bible study guys who I know had been praying for us throughout this entire situation (love these guys). Our friends Buddy and Annie sent us beautiful flowers.

It was at this moment that my perspective on flowers would be forever changed. I shared with Buddy of how much of a waste of money I felt like flowers were. You spend all of this money on these plants that you know will inevitably die, but Jude gave me a new appreciation for them. Just like Jude, even though they are only with us for a short time before they die, their momentary beauty can brighten up the room. I think I love flowers now.

Hugs (July 7)

We left the hospital and got settled back in our home, but not necessarily in our hearts. There were still a ton of emotions we were dealing with, but we knew we were going to be OK. Maggie was scheduled to attend Girls' Camp at Greenwood Hills for the first time. She shared that she was wrestling with a great deal of sadness, but that she still wanted to go to camp. My friend Mike bought us dinner which was the perfect act of kindness at just the right time. As I was watering our new plants including our "Jude Tree," my friend Charlie drove by. He was running late for work, but he quickly pulled over, hopped out, and gave me a hug. I desperately needed that.

Flowers & Friends – Part II (July 8)

We drove out to Greenwood Hills the next day to bring Maggie to Girls' Camp. It was awesome to connect with Scott and Andrea who were able to comfort Juli and I, having gone through the loss of their son recently. They were also dropping off their daughter for camp. We had the opportunity to pray for one another and were comforted by the reminder to rely on the Lord on the long road ahead. As we hung around the camp for a few days, we were excited to find out that they had sent us flowers. This was another reminder of my renewed appreciation for flowers and the beautiful thoughts of our son Jude that come to mind.

I also spent a decent amount of time preparing some thoughts and details around the memorial service for Jude that we were planning. This was tough and I was so glad we decided to give ourselves some time following Jude's birth and passing to hold some sort of service for him. I'm needing lots of time to process all of this.

Royal Feasts (July 9)

As Juli recovered from her C-section, I knew I was going to have to pick up my parenting game as she was instructed to take it easy with no heavy lifting (all of the diaper changing and bath times would fall on me). I also wanted to help by doing all of the cooking. Despite a short-lived desire in my younger years to become a professional chef, most people know that I cannot cook at all. As we spent the rest of the week at the family summer house while Maggie attended Girls' Camp, the Lord knew how to provide for us in areas that I was severely lacking. Outside of a few runs to Dunkin' Donuts for coffee and breakfast, the kitchen staff decided to send us leftover food from the camp every day. They were aware of what we had recently gone through and wanted to bless us in this way. What a blessing it was! The guy in charge of the meals that week was a professional chef, and we ate like royalty. A few local friends blessed us with other meals, including my friend Dan who had recently had a baby. Despite our continued sorrow, we were thrilled to have the opportunity to "rejoice with those who rejoice" (Romans 12:15). We also had a chance to enjoy the Elliott "Frank's Fried Turkey" special. If you know, you know.

The love and generosity of the family of God that was poured out on us confirmed what we already knew: God was going to carry us through the upcoming weeks, months, and even years.

Verse & Song #1 – Social Media Post (July 14)

Thank you everyone for your love, encouragement, support, and prayers. I hope that I can encourage each of you in return by sharing some of the ways we have been blessed during these last few months. Despite the difficulty in knowing Jude's diagnosis ahead of time, we learned to view that knowledge as a blessing from God as He used it as a way for us to 1.) Appreciate the months of pregnancy and time with Jude even more and 2.) Prepare our hearts by beginning the grieving process months before his passing.

So many things have helped us during this time, but two things in particular (in addition to our wonderful circle of friends and family): Verses & Songs.

VERSES...We read in Hebrews 4:12 that "the word of God is living and powerful, and sharper than any two-edged sword, piercing even to the division of soul and spirit, and of joints and marrow, and is a discerner of the thoughts and intents of the heart."

When we couldn't even discern our own thoughts and emotions, the Word of God became more "living" to us than ever before (if only we would ALWAYS let the Word speak to us so powerfully), as verses seemed to speak directly to us in our situation with Jude.

SONGS...In addition to the Beatles song that always pops into my head when thinking of Jude, so many other songs and "stories behind the songs" strengthened us in our faith as we walked this rocky road.

Some of these songs you may know, others you most likely will not, but our prayer is that WHATEVER trial you may be facing, no matter how trivial it may seem, that you would find hope. We have reminders all around us that God is a PERSONAL God who cares about us and loves us (as demonstrated through the sacrifice of His Son and the daily abundance of blessings He pours into our lives – Malachi 3:10). So many songs gave us the will to press on when we felt like giving up.

VERSES...
"Though He slay me, yet I will praise Him."
–Job 13:15
"The Lord gives, and the Lord takes away; Blessed be the name of the Lord."
–Job 1:21

SONG...
"Though You Slay Me" by Shane & Shane

Though You slay me, yet I will trust You.
Though You take from me, I will bless Your name.
Though You ruin me, still I will worship
And sing a song to the One who's all I need.

Also, thank you Maximilian Albrecht, for your friendship and for sharing this song with me. Love you, brother.

A Slip of the Text (July 17)

I'm realizing that it's the little things that will awaken the slumbering sadness. We were at my sister's house, and I was taking a nap with Augie while the rest of the family was at the pool. As my sister texted me to find out if I was coming soon, I wrote back, "Should I wake up Jude and come?" meaning to say "Augie." The tears started coming again and I knew this wasn't going to be easy.

Feelings (July 18)

Jim and Lisa just arrived at Kristin's house and their daughter Madison was lying on the floor. She was crying because her pacifier kept falling out. I kept putting it back in her mouth and she would calm down and just stare at me. I felt bad because I thought she wanted to be held, but I knew it would be too difficult emotionally for me to pick her up and hold her, and then I felt even worse for having those feelings.

JUDE'S MEMORIAL (JULY 23)

I knew I wouldn't be able to hold it together or keep my thoughts straight in my head, so I wrote down everything I wanted to share ahead of time. The family, friends, and coworkers that showed up in-person and joined online reminded us that people were praying for us and wanted to help us honor the brief life of our son…

Thank you all so much for coming.

We thank each and every one of you for the overwhelming love that you have shown to our family. We could not imagine having to go through this without two incredible things…our sovereign God who lovingly carried us on this journey by His mercy *and* the support of our loved ones, the family of God, our friends and family who reached out to talk, pray, cry and to just be with us.

As we've come together to remember the life of Jude, my mind goes back to a verse from Scripture that a wise friend recently shared with me. As I attended his young son's funeral, he reminded me of Job 1:21, where Job is reflecting on the overwhelming and heartbreaking loss of family and possession, pretty much everyone that he loved and everything that belonged to him, he says this, "Naked I came from my mother's womb, and naked shall I return there. The Lord gave and the Lord has taken away; Blessed be the name of the Lord." Amazed at my friend's faith, I shared with him that I couldn't imagine being in his shoes. And yet here we are.

I've realized through many conversations with many people that every situation is unique, but that so many people have suffered through the tragedy of miscarriage or stillbirth or the loss of a child. And yet, we don't always realize the pain and sorrow that our friends and family are going through.

I initially reflected on this verse as I considered all that our son August had gone through. And in the thoughts of "the Lord gives and the Lord takes away," I realized that August was indeed a gift given to us. Most of you know that he was born with significant health issues that required multiple surgeries and months in the hospital, all of this in the midst of a pandemic that initially shut everything down and delayed his treatment. I remember the joy we experienced in the outcome of all of August's circumstances, but I also noted at that time that if we can praise the name of God in the first part of that verse ("the Lord gives"), we would need to make a determined effort to praise the name of God in the latter part of that verse ("the Lord takes away"). Little did we know what we would soon face…And so we think of our son August as the Lord GIVING and of our son Jude as the Lord TAKING. However, in BOTH circumstances, we can declare, "Blessed be the name of the Lord!" And so, his name is a constant reminder to us…Jude, which means, to PRAISE!

Jude's diagnosis back in March gave us ample time to begin the process of preparing our hearts for loss. While we had seen God work wonders in our own lives and knew that He can do all things, we daily and faithfully prayed for a miracle, knowing full well that if it was His will, He could deliver Jude. However, we also knew that medically, if things proceeded as expected, we would need to not only prepare our own hearts, but also the hearts and minds of our children to say goodbye.

My prayer is that this morning I am able to speak on behalf of our entire family so I will share how each one of us has coped with the passing of Jude.

Maggie…Ever since Wesley was born, Maggie had been hoping for and praying for a baby sister. And brother after bother, she was still praying for that sister. When we found out that we were expecting a boy, Maggie was so disappointed. Upon sharing the diagnosis and likely outcome with Maggie, through tears, she cried that all she wanted was a baby brother. The wisdom in her questions and deep thoughts that she shared with Juli and I brought peace to our hearts in her level of maturity at her age. Her "Big Sister" status was finally achieved when she held her baby brother…As Maggie was thrilled to proudly hold Jude…the very first baby that she ever held while standing up. What an incredible big sister!

Wesley…Despite being our "too cool for school," tough little 6-year-old, Wesley's soft side and tender heart came out as he cherished every moment that he got to hold Jude. I have never seen such honest and heartfelt expressions of love than that morning as Wesley, with tears streaming down his face, held his baby brother.

Dexter…He was our big thinker and asker of many, many deep questions…As his little mind tried to grasp these big and heavy things, he was fully aware of the expected outcome as he was never shy to tell his friends that his little baby brother was going to die. While his comments often seemed disassociated from any emotions, he seemed to be the one who was always hugging, kissing, and rubbing his mommy's belly and enjoying Jude's presence while in the womb.

August…I believe Augie understood a lot more than we realize. When we would pray as a family, in the rare instance that we forgot to pray for Jude, Augie would yell "No!" followed by "Baby Jude for a miracle!" He would often point to Juli's belly and call for his little brother. One of his favorite books was called *Big Brother*. He was often thinking of Jude. On occasion, he would point to my belly and ask, "baby Jude?" to which I would have to explain that I was just getting fatter.

When Juli was putting August into his crib on the night that Jude was born, Juli asked him what song he would like to sing. For some reason, Augie said he wanted to sing Happy Birthday to his baby brother which was not one of our typical bedtime songs. Sure enough, Jude would arrive a few hours later.

For Juli...This pregnancy brought us through a wide range of emotions. Normally, the anticipation of the arrival of a newborn baby is something that families look forward to. While we looked forward to his arrival, we knew that outside of a miracle, we would also have to say our goodbyes. His arrival would ultimately mean the end of his time with us on earth. Some people even asked (with every good intention), given our knowledge of Jude's condition, if the situation made Juli want to CHOOSE to be pregnant forever, to which Juli, after a *very* brief hesitation, promptly said, "No." We understood what they meant and actually sympathized with that perspective as we really never wanted to say goodbye and truly cherished every kick, every punch, every single moment of this pregnancy more than any other.

Jude's life has left a lasting impact on me personally and I believe it can be summed up in a letter that I wrote to him shortly after receiving the news of his diagnosis, lying awake in bed, unable to sleep being overwhelmed with sadness.

"Dear Jude...Before we even get to officially meet, you don't even know how much you've changed me...I hope and pray, and by faith, I already know how much of a better father you have made me...When I consider all of the bedtime stories we won't get to read, all of the backyard catches we won't get to have, all of the hugs we won't get to share, I've been reminded of your brothers and sister who I still have with me...to make those memories with. I'm reminded to give them more time in honor of the time I won't get to spend with you. Thank you for making me a better father. I pray I can live up to the challenge that you've placed in my heart. I love you so much and I will miss you. Love, Daddy."

And this brings me to what I have sincerely prayed will be the lasting testimony of Jude's brief time on earth. That he would make us consider our CHOICES. Since the diagnosis we were presented with choices...

At CHOP our choices were...
1. Clinical Trial
2. "Interrupt the Pregnancy"
3. Continue to Full Term

We have shared previously our reasons for our decision, but we obviously chose to carry Jude until delivery, being told that this would be the more difficult route, emotionally and perhaps even physically.

We were presented with CHOICES during our visits with the Pediatric Palliative Care team at MMC…

> C-section or not? When to schedule? Family and/or photographer to come in or not? How long would we keep his body after he passed? What keepsakes and memories did we want? Funeral arrangements?

Choices throughout the pregnancy in how we would respond emotionally and spiritually…

> —Would we grow angry & bitter towards God for taking away our son?
> —Or would we echo the words of Job and praise God?

Despite Job being advised to curse God, we see that his response was to fall down and worship in the midst of such loss.

In the Word of God, we do not read much on children who have died, but as the prayer that was read earlier states, "Your Word says little of such mysteries, and yet, in what is revealed, we find good reason to take heart."

In Israel's history, King David also had a choice in how he would respond upon hearing that his son had died. In 2 Samuel 12: 20-23 we read:

"So, David arose from the ground, washed and anointed himself, and went into the house of the Lord and worshiped. Then he went to his own house; and when he requested, they set food before him, and he ate. Then his servants said to him, 'What is this that you have done? You fasted and wept for the child while he was alive, but when the child died, you arose and ate food.' And he said, 'While the child was alive, I fasted and wept; for I said, 'Who can tell whether the Lord will be gracious to me, that the child may live?' But now he is dead; why should I fast? Can I bring him back again? I shall go to him, but he shall not return to me.'"

What did David *choose* to do upon hearing the news. He *chose* to worship. Juli and I took a page out of David's playbook as we asked ourselves, "Can we do anything to bring him back?" The obvious answer is no. But we choose to move forward by worshipping God, with the same confidence of David, that Jude is with our Savior in heaven…he may not return to us, but we shall go to him!

We would be foolish to think that by simply *saying* we believe in a sovereign God who is in complete control of every situation, *without actually believing it*, would bring any sort of true peace.

168

What hope, what comfort, what peace is there in saying we have our confidence in something that we do not even believe is real? This type of self-deception would be the cruelest form of self-inflicted pain that one could put on themselves.

But we share with you our hope in a personal God who created Jude and granted us the privilege of caring for him for a very short time because we have seen His goodness. We have experienced the incredible life, with all of its ups and downs, that God has blessed us with.

We have been able to repeat from the depths of our own hearts what the psalmist said, "Oh, taste and see that the Lord is good; Blessed is the man who trusts in Him" (Psalm 34:8).

Jude never had the chance to make any choices, but we firmly believe from Scripture, which we hold to be the Word of God that Jude is in our Savior's presence right now. Jesus said in Matthew 19:14, "Let the little children come to Me, for of such is the kingdom of heaven." The Word of God makes it even more clear to each and every one of us who is capable of making a choice, that we must choose…

My biggest prayer this morning is that Jude's life would cause each of you to not only carefully consider all of your choices, but to consider the most important CHOICE of all…To answer the exact same question that Pontius Pilate asked just prior to handing over our Savior to die on a cross for our sins, "What should I do with Jesus Christ?" Will you accept Him or reject Him?

Despite what this world tries to teach us, our salvation, our forgiveness, our eternal destination is not dependent on our own good works, our efforts to meet the standard that a holy God requires because none of us could meet that standard of perfection. As Ephesians 2:8-9 reminds us, "For by grace you have been saved through faith, and that not of yourselves, it is the gift of God, not of works, lest anyone should boast."

I pray that the passing of Jude would cause all of us to consider the brevity of life and that the only way to forgiveness and peace with God is through placing our faith and confidence in the death and resurrection of the Lord Jesus Christ.

May we carefully consider the words of the psalm that were just read as if our lives depended on them, because they do, "For you, Lord, are good, and ready to forgive, and abundant in mercy to all those who call upon You" (Psalm 86:5).

This is indeed a sad day, a reminder of the sorrow that we feel with the loss of Jude, but please don't feel sorry for us. We don't sorrow as a family without hope. May his death be an invitation to you to choose to share the joy and hope and comfort and peace that Jude is experiencing now. That all who know Jesus as Savior can genuinely experience in part, today, but fully in a future day.

Thank you to our friends and family that knew exactly what to share with us in our moment of deepest sorrow. Whether it was a Bible verse that was just what we needed to hear or a word of encouragement or a prayer, we are sincerely grateful.

Thank you so much to our friends and family that perhaps didn't know what to say, but just reached out to let us know that they didn't know what to say. It meant the world to us that your love for us overcame your concern of not having the right words.

Thank you to our church family at Fifth Avenue Chapel for being the real and genuine display of the love of Christ in our lives as you comforted us in so many real and practical ways.

Thank you to my extended work family at Monmouth Medical Center. We could not have asked for a better team to help us welcome our little guy into this world for his short stay.

Thank you to Juli…the strongest woman I know…who showed her strength when I was unable to do so and helped keep the calm in the chaos. I love you, Juli.

Thank you to God who has truly blessed us with a peace that passes all understanding as He has carried us through these challenging months as we prepared to say hello and goodbye to our son.

Thank you to our Lord and Savior Jesus Christ. Thank You for giving Your life so that we might receive the forgiveness of sins and for welcoming Jude to heaven. We miss him so incredibly much, but we know he is in good hands as he rests in the arms of Jesus. We will see you soon.

My Heart Yearns Within Me (July 24)

"For I know that my Redeemer lives,
And He shall stand at last on the earth;
And after my skin is destroyed, this I know,
That in my flesh I shall see God,
Whom I shall see for myself,

And my eyes shall behold, and not another.
How my heart yearns within me!"
–Job 19:25-27

I cried more on Sunday than at the memorial service. I read a book last night with the kids about our desire for heaven and how it should really be a desire to be with Jesus. Yes, our desire to be reunited with Jude is a good one, but our hearts should yearn to see Jesus. My friend, Craig, read from the above verses and then we sang "Before the Throne of God Above." This was the song that I sang to each of our kids in the hospital right after they were born, and it hit me at that moment that I did not get the chance to sing this song to Jude. This was the "magic" bedtime song that, if I sung it twice through to Maggie when she was a baby, she would always fall asleep by the end. But more a cure for insomnia, the words point us to the "great High Priest whose name is Love."

I shared at this morning's Remembrance Meeting thoughts regarding the depth of the love of our God. Juli's parents had come up to visit for the memorial service and I thought about how when Juli's dad is visiting, Wesley completely ignores me and follows his Papa around. I asked him how come when Papa is here, it's like I don't even exist anymore? He replied, "Because Papa loves me more than you do!"

What?! I really hope that Wesley understands the depth of my love for him, but it could never compare with the love that God has for us. The fact that God loves us more than anything should make our hearts yearn for Him more than anything else.

Back & Forth (July 25)

"It is good to give thanks to the LORD,
And to sing praises to Your name, O Most High;
To declare Your lovingkindness in the morning,
And Your faithfulness every night."
–Psalm 92:1-2

To declare His lovingkindness is to look forward to seeing the Lord's goodness through the upcoming day in anticipation and expectation. To declare His faithfulness at night is to look back on all His fulfilled promises. One looks forward, the other looks back.

We had a full fun-filled day at Hurricane Harbor, riding on the lazy river after Dexter complained that he didn't want to go on big slides. As we relaxed and floated in the tube, I realized I would never get a chance to do this with Jude, but it also made me think of His eternal resting place.

Roommates & Brothers (July 27)

I had the chance to catch up with my friend, Jake, on the phone for a few hours. We were reminiscing about the good ole days spending summers at Greenwood Hills as roommates on summer staff. He shared how he was able to share our story with his kids in letting Jude go to full-term as an example of how we can make choices and live in light of what Scripture teaches.

Lord, thank you so much for brothers in Christ who are able to encourage us in the dark times and lift us up in prayer when we need it most.

Verse & Song #2 – Social Media Post (July 28)

VERSE...
"Be anxious for nothing, but in everything by prayer and supplication, with thanksgiving, let your requests be made known to God; and the peace of God, which surpasses all understanding, will guard your hearts and minds through Christ Jesus."
–Philippians 4:6-7

As Juli and I drove back from CHOP this past March, the cloudy and rainy, dark and gloomy weather matched our mood. They had just confirmed Jude's diagnosis and we had just finished a meal at a fine Italian restaurant to match our disappointment (my chicken and pasta were both severely undercooked and painfully overpriced).

On the drive back as we tried to process everything, I heard the below song for the very first time. While I listened to the song, I began to pray for a miracle.

After Jude's passing, the music video for this has changed my perspective on how God was working in our lives. While the miracle we were hoping for was not in His plan, the story presented in the video suggested that, despite the experienced loss, a family can grow even stronger through such tragedy...and perhaps the miracle we were longing for was not the particular miracle that God wanted to actually give us.

I have recently heard of a number of families that were devastatingly broken apart after experiencing personal tragedies. God has indeed given us a peace as we have brought our honest and sincere requests before Him and used this tragedy as a way to draw our family closer to Him and closer to each other.

I believe that God can provide you and your family with a PEACE that "will GUARD your HEARTS and MINDS" as you face whatever trials you are in the midst of.

SONG...
"In Jesus Name (God of Possible)" by Katy Nichole

I pray for your healing
That circumstances will change
I pray that the fear inside will flee in Jesus' name
I pray that a breakthrough
Would happen today
I pray miracles over your life in Jesus' name
I pray for revival
For restoration of faith
I pray that the dead will come alive in Jesus' name
In Jesus' name

Facing the Negative (July 29)

Francis Schaeffer's *True Spirituality* (1971, p. 23):

"Is it not true that our thoughts, our prayers for ourselves and those we love and our conversations are almost entirely aimed at getting rid of the negative at any cost, rather than praying that the negatives might be faced in the proper attitude?"

The Moon is Always Round (July 30)

As I was listening to Maggie's heartbeat with the doppler, Augie came into the room. When I asked him whose heartbeat we were hearing, he responded, "Baby Jude!" When we were at Jim and Lisa's house and saw a picture of Brooklyn holding Wesley as a baby, we asked Augie who Brooklyn was holding…. "Baby Jude!"

Our friends, Brian and Angie, were visiting from out-of-town and we simply had the most encouraging conversation we have had in a while. They sent us a book entitled *The Moon is Always Round,* which truly was a blessing to not only Juli and I, but the kids as well. We were still in the baby stages of learning how to talk about this with our kids and this book seemed to put things into perspective for all of us.

Empty Hands (August 3)

In speaking of our salvation, Francis Schaeffer writes:

"A man can never be justified on the basis of his own faith. Through all of salvation the only basis is the finished work of Jesus Christ on the cross in history. Faith is the empty hand, the *instrument* by which we accept God's free gift. Faith is simply believing God. It is not a leap in the dark. It is ceasing to call God a liar and believing Him" (2011, p. 68).

It is not about how strong our faith is, but how strong the One is in whom we put our faith. How true this is of our salvation, and yet, I can't stop thinking of how true this is through this time of loss.

Lord, help me to hold up empty hands towards You and be willing and ready to receive whatever You have to offer us.

Verse & Song #3 – Social Media Post (August 7)

VERSE...
"Unless the LORD had been my help,
My soul would soon have settled in silence.
If I say, 'My foot slips,' Your mercy, O LORD, will hold me up.
In the multitude of my anxieties within me, Your comforts delight my soul."
–Psalm 94:17-19

In recent months, Juli and I often did not have words to comfort each other in certain moments and it wasn't that we didn't know where to turn for help, we were just so overwhelmed with sorrow that we just had to sit in silence.

BUT...

We held onto the reality of these verses...

WHEN our souls were left speechless,
THEN the Lord was our help.

WHEN we slipped,
THEN the mercy of God held us up.

WHEN we were overwhelmed by anxiety,
THEN His comforts delighted our soul.

...God is soooo good even when life is not...

SONG...
"No Tomorrow" by Wolves at the Gate

This overwhelming weight that covers up my eyes
Is telling me that mercy is a lie that's in disguise
Just like a million stones are strung around my neck
As I drown in the abyss I'm falling till I
Feel the wings of mercy lift me up and carry me

We are left with silent sorrow, no tomorrow. Lost, unknown
Until You hear me screaming out now for Your love

You're counting down my sins, each one a grain of sand
They're filling up a desert as You hold them in Your hand
You carry it away and bear it all alone
Every sin You've taken as Your own

Surprise (August 7)

We went up to Massachusetts to visit some friends and celebrate our friend Shannon's birthday. When Shannon came into the surprise party, Juli saw her and started to cry. When I asked her why, she couldn't quite pin down the exact reason. Perhaps it was because the last time we were supposed to see Shannon was when she was planning on coming to Jude's memorial service, but she couldn't make it due to unexpected car trouble. Either way, we had a wonderful time catching up with friends. Many of whom we had not seen in a very long time.

I had the opportunity to share our family's testimony of God's faithfulness and the power of His Word over the last few years of our lives at the chapel that weekend. I pray that it was as helpful and encouraging to the saints at the chapel there as it was surprisingly therapeutic for me to share.

Lord, thank You for Your faithfulness through all of the unexpected events of the past three years.

Verse & Song #4 – Social Media Post (August 8)

Anniversary Edition

VERSE...
"Whereas you do not know what will happen tomorrow. For what is your life? It is even a vapor that appears for a little time and then vanishes away."
–James 4:14

"So, teach us to number our days,
That we may gain a heart of wisdom."
–Psalm 90:12

Today marks our 14th Wedding Anniversary. It's a bittersweet day as this was also Jude's due date. It was a date that we had mixed emotions about. A day we anticipated yet feared. Over the weekend, we went to pick up his birth and death certificate. It's little reminders like these that break our hearts, but also cause us to rejoice in the beautiful minutes we had with our precious son who we love and miss dearly.

But we have been reminded that despite the brevity of Jude's life, our lives will be forever changed. While holding those two certificates which marked the beginning and end of his life, I thought about the verses above which remind us that in light of eternity, our lives are very short (James 4:14). Some decisions we make have eternal consequences (e.g. what will I do with Jesus Christ? Do to others as you would have them do to you - Matthew 7:12), which are MUCH more important than decisions we make with temporary consequences (e.g. do I get the pumpkin or glazed munchkins at Dunkin?...and yes...pumpkin munchkins are back).

As the old saying goes (I think it's an old saying), Psalm 90:12 reminds us to not simply COUNT our DAYS, but to MAKE our days COUNT.

The prophet Samuel set up stones as a memorial to God's deliverance of Israel. He called it "Ebenezer" which means "stone of help." The little reminders we have on days like this are our own personal ebenezers...small reminders...little memorials...of where our help comes from. I've recently been reminded of this by a song that has touched me deeply in recent weeks. Thank you, Lisa Cags, for sharing this song with us.

God was good to us 14 years ago when Juli and I said, "I do." He's still just as good today! Love you, Juli!

SONG...
"Just as Good" by Chris Renzema

And You're still just as good as when I met You
You're still just as kind, don't let me forget that You're
Still the same God that led me through the fire
You're still the same God who separates the waters
Come do what only You can do
God, I need You
And I will build an altar
And stack it stone by stone
'Cause every Ebenezer says I've never been alone
My faith will surely falter
But that don't change what You've done
'Cause every Ebenezer points to where my help comes from

Weird, Uncontrollable Beast (August 10)

I finished reading Steve Peifer's *A Dream So Big*, a book that a friend from college sent me. This is a story of one family's journey after losing their son to a genetic disorder resulting in kidney and lung issues. They lost him after eight days and on their path to finding purpose, Steven ended up moving to Africa and developing a program to help feed over 20,000 Kenyan children across 35 different public schools. As he struggled within his own sorrow of losing a son, he shared that "Grief is such a weird, uncontrollable beast. You never know when or where or how it's going to pop up and demand its due. The triggers for my wife were different from what they were for me" (Pfeifer, 2013, p. 45).

I couldn't have described what I was feeling better than how Steve tells it below:

"The only way I can think to describe my life after Stephen died is that it was like driving a car that had slipped into neutral. I had my foot on the gas, but it didn't go anywhere. The engine roared, but nothing else worked anymore. Then we came here (Rift Valley Academy), which has shown me the truth in one of my favorite verses: 'He who seeks to find his own life will lose it. He who seeks to lose his own life will find it.' When Stephen died, I felt like I lost my own life. Africa helped me find it again" (Peifer, 2013, p. 130).

To Test & To Heal (August 17)

I had another opportunity to share our family's testimony at my wife's old church in Florida. In addition to what I had shared with our friends up north, I shared more evidence that I knew God was going to continue to reveal Himself and His purpose for my life through His Word. Too often I neglected spending time in the one Book that actually has the power to give life. As I continued through the book of Psalms, I found two verses (or better yet, they found me) that summed up the power of God's Word on our lives:

"Until the time that his word came to pass,
The word of the Lord **TESTED** him."
–Psalm 105:19

"He sent His word and **HEALED** them,
And delivered them from their destructions."
–Psalm 107:20

The Word of God can both *test* and *heal* simultaneously. Not giving up and not giving in to hopelessness and despair felt next to impossible. It truly felt like a season of testing when the Lord was commanding us in His Word to trust in Him, but from my self-centered perspective, He wasn't giving me any reason to do so. Yet, while we found the call to live in submission to His Word a very difficult test indeed, we saw the healing that came through those same words that God used to test us.

Lord, thank you for Your Word that teaches us to trust You in the moments of testing, yet also brings the healing that we need when we feel that the testing is more than we can bear.

Thank You Letter – Monmouth Medical Center

Hi Eric and Darla,

This past summer, our family went through an event that we wish no family ever had to go through. After receiving tremendous care at the brand-new Anne Vogel Family Care and Wellness Center (whose facilities are almost as beautiful as the people who work there), we learned that our son would most likely be born with a condition that was not compatible with life after birth (Bilateral Renal Agenesis). We consider it a blessing to have learned of this condition prior to our son's birth as it gave us time to prepare. A number of coworkers immediately directed us to Susan Dulczak and Maria Graminski in the Pediatric Palliative Care program at Monmouth Medical Center. Knowing that the upcoming months would be incredibly difficult for us, their team provided us with the guidance and resources that we needed to create a birth plan for our son. We would have felt hopelessly lost without their direction and we are indebted to their service and continued support.

Soon after, we connected with the PMAD team at the new family care center (once again…beautiful building, even more beautiful people) where Carolyn Stack and Seton provided incredible support to my wife, Juli. We were not sure what to anticipate emotionally through all of this, but it was great to know that this care team was available to us leading up to our son's birth and for the months to follow.

In the closing hours of the evening of the Fourth of July, once all of the fireworks had ended, our son decided it was time to make his grand entrance. I was working the nightshift at RWJ New Brunswick, so my wife was assisted by the wonderful MMC Emergency Department staff up to Labor & Delivery as I raced down Route 18.

Jude Phineas Cagliostro arrived on July 5, 2022, at 2:57 a.m. Susan Dulczak's team put us in touch with an organization called Joan's Reach that provided us with wonderful resources to prepare for Jude's birth, including a photographer who works with families dealing with infant loss. Working with Jennifer Angersbach, we were able to coordinate the approvals for getting this photographer and our children up to our room before Jude's arrival. I was able to arrive shortly before Dr. Smith brought Juli back for a C-Section. Dr. Smith and her team (Dr. Pompliano, Dr. Jackson, and Sam the midwife) were amazing in walking us through the difficult decisions that we had to make along the way.

All the while praying for a miracle and believing whole-heartedly that God could intervene if He so desired, we knew that medically speaking if nature ran its course, we would have to say our goodbyes to our son shortly after his birth.

Dr. Qualtar was extremely helpful during our meetings with the Pediatric Palliative Care team, but in her absence, Dr. Kale was our NICU specialist that night who walked us through these emotional moments. Dr. Harshani (OBGYN Resident) provided wonderful care as well.

The nursing leadership team and the staff on the Labor & Delivery unit could not have been more awesome! Special shout-out to Sarah who spent multiple days with us and worked so well with our kids. The staff gave our family the time that we needed to say goodbye to Jude and helped us create a variety of memories and keepsakes to bring home with us. A million thanks go out to Sarah, Jen, Nicki Altenau, Nicole Lamoureux, Ann Marie, Tsipora, Melissa, Dana, Juliana, Jessica, Dawn, Xenia, Amanda, Kim and Sharon S. I apologize as I know I am leaving many names out (including departments such as dietary, housekeeping, security, etc.), but we wanted to express our sincerest gratitude to this team for being a huge part of our family's healing journey.

We are humbled in sharing this, but a number of people commented on how well we were handling this deeply personal loss and many of them attributed it to the strength of our faith. Personally, my wife and I could only respond by simply sharing that it was not the *strength* of our faith, but *who* we put our faith in. We had confidence in God and in our Lord and Savior Jesus Christ that He would carry us through this incredibly difficult journey, but it was amazing to see that He did so by giving us the best team of care providers that anyone could ask for. We could not have dreamed of a more qualified group of professional and compassionate individuals than the ones who cared for us. They turned an impossible situation into one filled with blessing and hope.

Monmouth Medical Center has a very special place in my heart. Not only was it my birthplace in which my life was saved as a premature baby in NICU, but it is where all of our children were born. Not only have our family and friends received trustworthy, quality care here for decades, but it has been an honor to call MMC my place of employment for the last 15 years. I recently visited the new coffee shop in the parking garage and the barista was so surprised at the attitude of all of the MMC employees that it led him to ask me, "Why is everyone so happy here?" I told him that I believe many employees see Monmouth Medical Center as a *family*…A place where they have grown as professionals, developed relationships with coworkers, and poured their hearts and souls into their patients.

Despite our loss, we rejoice in knowing that the memories we cherish with our son are all thanks to the incredible team at Monmouth Medical Center. Thank you once again for everything!

With grateful hearts,
Joe and Juli Cagliostro (with Maggie, Wesley, Dexter, and August)

Thank You Letter – Fifth Avenue Chapel

Dear chapel family,

Juli and I would like to express our sincerest gratitude for your kindness and love over the past few months. With the arrival and departure of Jude earlier this year, God has made His faithful presence so evident to us through the compassion, generosity, and thoughtfulness of all of the saints here at Fifth Avenue Chapel. While the journey has been difficult and will continue to be difficult, we are incredibly grateful for the prayers, messages, kindness, flowers and gifts that all of you have so lovingly poured out on us.

Thank you for your kindness in helping us remember Jude with a memorial service held here at the chapel. We were so blessed to have so many of you contribute your efforts to remembering our son. We will never forget your support during these hard, but special days. Thank you for praying with us and sharing words of encouragement and the Word of God with us. Thank you for living out Romans 12:15 and weeping with us as we wept. May we continue to rejoice now together as we continue on in faithfulness to our Lord and Savior Jesus Christ who has proven Himself faithful to us (2 Timothy 2:13).

Trusting in Him,

Joe & Juli Cagliostro (with Maggie, Wesley, Dexter, and August)

"Through the Lord's mercies we are not consumed, because His compassions fail not. They are new every morning; great is Your faithfulness. 'The Lord is my portion,' says my soul, 'Therefore I hope in Him!' The Lord is good to those who wait for Him, to the soul who seeks Him. It is good that one should hope and wait quietly for the salvation of the Lord."
–Lamentations 3:22-26

"Blessed be the God and Father of our Lord Jesus Christ, the Father of mercies and God of all comfort, who comforts us in all our tribulation, that we may be able to comfort those who are in any trouble, with the comfort with which we ourselves are comforted by God."
–2 Corinthians 1:3-4

"You will keep him in perfect peace, whose mind is stayed on You, because he trusts in You."
–Isaiah 26:3

Verse & Song #5 – Social Media Post (October 1)

VERSE...
"He heals the broken-hearted and binds up their wounds."
–Psalm 147:3

Some days are tougher than others, but God has given our family the strength, healing and endurance to rest in Him and press on. No matter what sorrows or troubles you have recently endured or even if you are in the middle of tremendous heartbreak, God promises in His Word that He can heal you. We have experienced first-hand the healing that is promised in Psalm 147:3.

Emotions come and go like the changing of seasons, but the Word of God endures and reminds us that there is purpose in the pain...there is healing in the hurt.

In 2 Corinthians 6:10, Paul describes himself as "sorrowful, yet always rejoicing." The passing of Jude has been tough, but we can identify with Paul because even though this sorrow sticks around, our eternal hope is in Christ. Through everything, we have felt the reality that "weeping may last for the night, but joy comes in the morning" (Psalm 30:5).

In Matthew 5:4, Jesus said, "Blessed are those who mourn, for they shall be comforted." While every individual, every family, every man, every woman, every child mourns differently, in our unique journeys we have truly felt blessed. We have been comforted and learned that God's healing is an incredible thing to rest in.

We had the opportunity to sing the below song as a family at Jude's memorial service, and I share it here because it really was our anthem during those difficult months and the words continue to be an encouragement to us in the harder days. Thank you everyone for praying with us, talking with us, and walking with us. Many of you have carried our burden with us and made it bearable (Galatians 6:2). Thank you all for your love and support. You have helped turn our sorrow into a source of joy and hope as we trust in the One who heals the broken-hearted.

SONG...
"Come What May" by We Are Messengers

Sometimes sorrow is the door to peace
Sometimes heartache is the gift I need
You're faithful, faithful in all things...

There is deep joy that You give to me
Where hurt meets the healing is a holy thing
I see goodness, Your goodness in all things…

In every high, in every low
On mountain tops, down broken roads
You're still my rock, my hope remains
I'll rest in the arms of Jesus
Come what may

Near – Social Media Post (May 7, 2023)

For all of the moms who have suffered through the pain and sorrow of the loss of a child at any stage, the following Scripture and song have been comforting to us and we pray that you, too, will find comfort in the nearness of God as offered in Jesus:

"But now in Christ Jesus you who once were far off have been brought near by the blood of Christ."
–Ephesians 2:13

"Always" by JJ Heller
https://youtu.be/QxEQI96PErU

"The Lord is near to the brokenhearted and saves the crushed in spirit."
–Psalm 34:18

One Year – Social Media Post (July 5, 2023)

One year since we got to say hello.

Exactly one year since we had to say goodbye.

We were truly blessed to be able to share those brief early morning minutes with Jude. As we remember those precious moments, we wanted to thank all of our friends and family for your continued love, support, and prayers that helped us through the most difficult time of our lives.

God used this past year to not only draw us closer to Him, but to strengthen our family as we learned to become fully dependent on a God who we believe has our best interest in mind.

He has proven Himself faithful, and we have no doubt that He will continue to sustain us (Isaiah 46:4). We truly have the greatest Savior who has blessed us with the most incredible family, friends, church, neighbors, coworkers...we can't thank you enough...you're awesome and we love you!

"You've Already Won" by Shane & Shane

There's peace that outlasts darkness
Hope that's in the blood
There's future grace that's mine today
That Jesus Christ has won
So I can face tomorrow
For tomorrow's in Your hands
All I need, you will provide
Just like you always have

I'm fighting a battle
You've already won
No matter what comes my way
I will overcome
I don't know what you're doing
But I know what you've done
I'm fighting a battle
You've already won.

RESOURCES & REFERENCES

As a help for those who find themselves searching for the right words to comfort a loved one during a time of personal loss or suffering, please check out the "For They Shall Be Comforted" episode of the *Wisdom at the Gate* series on Greenwood Hills Camps & Conferences' YouTube channel. I was invited to share our story along with how God comforted us and what we learned about how to best comfort others. The below "Practical Pointers" were shared, but for context and to listen to the entire episode, please go to:

https://www.youtube.com/watch?v=D3vz03mr1_4&list=PLylwK3UNtUem
VzuuUnFXhMdpMSMGudCi0&index=7

1. Recognize the Hurt (Job 2:11)
2. Acknowledge the Hurt (Job 2:12)
3. Don't Say Anything (Job 2:13)
4. Say Something (Proverbs 25:11)
5. Share Scripture/Song/Sermon
6. You Don't Have to Have All of the Answers (Mark 15:34)
7. Ask if They Want to Talk About It
8. Don't Put a Time Limit on Their Healing (Ecclesiastes 3:4)
9. Avoid Criticism
10. Consider Your Audience (Hebrews 10:24)
11. Point Them to the Right Resources (1 Peter 5:7)
12. Check-In with Co-Mourners (1 Peter 3:7)
13. Customize Your Comfort

Links

The Life of Jude
https://www.youtube.com/watch?v=eQIEVsuK7Hc

Jude's Memorial Service
https://www.youtube.com/watch?v=diRdIfcRR0g

August and Jude's Playlist
https://music.youtube.com/playlist?list=PLTnv3s0xVTzVRjUYBJR2IfvhbV
m56CJMp&si=6_SFAAjAm3wbPjQm

Organizations

"Joan's Reach." *Joan's Reach*, www.joansreach.org/. Accessed 4 July 2022.

Zinser, Ashley. "Remembrance Portraits." *Now I Lay Me Down to Sleep*, 15 May 2024, www.nowilaymedowntosleep.org/, Photos of Jude.

Books & Websites

Cagliostro, Joseph. (2023, January 22). *The gathering storm on human life*. [Video]. YouTube. https://www.youtube.com/watch?v=2NoNoXPQMDI

Gibson, Jonathan, and Joe Hox. *The Moon Is Always Round*. LSC-NewGrowthPress, 2019.

Gooding, D. W. *True to the Faith*. Myrtlefield House, 2013.

"Growing Christians Ministries." *Growing Christians Ministries*, www.growingchristians.org/. Accessed 25 June 2022.

"Into Your Bible Ministries." *Into Your Bible Ministries*, www.intoyourbible.org/. Accessed 18 June 2022.

Pearcey, Nancy. *Love Thy Body: Answering Hard Questions about Life and Sexuality*. Baker Books, 2019.

Peifer, Steve, and Gregg Lewis. *A Dream so Big: Our Unlikely Journey to End the Tears of Hunger*. Zondervan, 2013.

Peterson, Andrew. *Adorning the Dark*. B&H Publishing Group, 2019.

Peterson, Andrew. *The God of the Garden: Thoughts on Creation, Culture, and the Kingdom*. B&H Publishing, 2021.

Schaeffer, Francis A. *True Spirituality*. Crossway Books, 2020.

Schumacher, Eric. *Ours*. The Good Book Company, 2022.

Smith, Angie. *I Will Carry You: The Sacred Dance of Grief and Joy*. B&H Publishing, 2010.

Songs (in order of appearance)

Wavorly. "Time I Understood?" *Conquering the Fear of Flight*, Provident, 2007.
https://music.youtube.com/watch?v=3vdYoMMLY-I&si=leHbSmNjT14OfuVH.

Twenty One Pilots. "Ride." *Blurryface,* Fueled by Ramen, 2015.
https://music.youtube.com/watch?v=w1Smzzw_w7Q&si=E_zW8C KOALvMrYdb.

Rend Collective. "Life Is Beautiful." *Good News*, Rend Family Records, 2018.
https://music.youtube.com/watch?v=KsSRCmlosQ0&si=YSzQn3hpz ExvcO1V.

David Crowder Band. "Because He Lives." *Give Us Rest*, Sixsteps, 2012.
https://music.youtube.com/watch?v=WMzRTvYaUGU&si=bAgPvSI kltx2fQwJ.

Casting Crowns. "Praise You in This Storm." *Lifesong*, Provident, 2005.
https://music.youtube.com/watch?v=nBj9NLPa2cs&si=f19Z9dGz-T5tb9pd.

Leeland. "Way Maker (Live)." *Single,* Integrity, 2019.
https://music.youtube.com/watch?v=cxtoDBnVu7I&si=Vzvjf1Tf0DI ppdl6.

Tauren Wells. "Trenches." *Citizen of Heaven*, Provident, 2020.
https://music.youtube.com/watch?v=jfIvPBjVhvg&si=84XFUsxbv1 M0wT_y.

We Are Messengers. "Magnify." *We Are Messengers*, Word Entertainment, 2016.
https://music.youtube.com/watch?v=HTE6aJBpKTM&si=BLm-gu9bWOYN6Y54.

Chris Rice. "It Is Well With My Soul." *Peace Like a River: The Hymns Project*,
Fair Trade Services, 2006.
https://music.youtube.com/watch?v=_CKerrMYq1M&si=YU77upnv wBHRiMA9.

Hillary Scott & the Scott Family. "Thy Will." *Love Remains*, Capitol, 2016.
https://music.youtube.com/watch?v=tjqfbKcN8Ms&si=L6ZF-eiI2o2Z-ZRg.

Katy Nichole. "In Jesus Name (God of Possible)." *Katy Nichole*, Centricity, 2022. https://music.youtube.com/watch?v=ihrUIPfvTh8&si=rWJWoQCfqp4Btt46.

Jordan St. Cyr. "Fires." *Fires*, BEC Recordings, 2020. https://music.youtube.com/watch?v=Y0TZXVo-6lA&si=PzvIFF1TV-w4Y73d.

Citizens & Saints. "I Am Living in a Land of Death." *Citizens*, Mars Hill, 2013. https://music.youtube.com/watch?v=Gnl0SXWfUbs&si=pZaJ7VRFSUd465TL.

Jordan St. Cyr. "Let Go, Let God." *Jordan St. Cyr*, BEC Recordings, 2023. https://music.youtube.com/watch?v=zOykSZrHLtE&si=DmwjG6NDq6Rtpygh.

Brave Saint Saturn. "Estrella." *The Light of Things Hoped For*, 2003. https://music.youtube.com/watch?v=qTEmjjSemy4&si=oeYu85Br4ox5JzhW.

Vertical Worship. "Yes I Will." *Yes I Will*, Provident, 2018. https://music.youtube.com/watch?v=2q4aZWGiXOQ&si=d4ZL8EnHmZ7aXIJt.

Shane & Shane. "Though You Slay Me." *Bring Your Nothing*, Fair Trade, 2013. https://music.youtube.com/watch?v=qyUPz6_TciY&si=VmANc7bxIhjcP8zU.

Wolves at the Gate. "No Tomorrow." *Eulogies*, Solid State Records, 2022. https://music.youtube.com/watch?v=Ff5qUSEyMf8&si=UtVkr0ROApVKv-I1.

Chris Renzema. "Just as Good." *Get Out of the Way of Your Own Heart*, CM, 2021. https://music.youtube.com/watch?v=_pFhiuX2Gjw&si=PFK_pii8ca5ImjSv

We Are Messengers. "Come What May." *Wholehearted*, Word, 2021. https://music.youtube.com/watch?v=r2czLnjCa-Q&si=9i2dCY9Uti-Uyya9.

Shane & Shane. "You've Already Won." *You've Already Won*, TWI, 2023. https://music.youtube.com/watch?v=CACOsoOQWY4&si=24wu-FzSWw7tszVT.

AUGUST

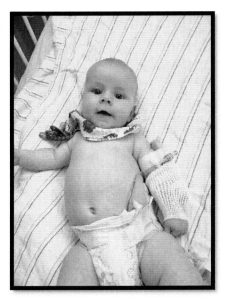

After Nephrostomy Tubes, Before Stent Placement (June 15, 2020)

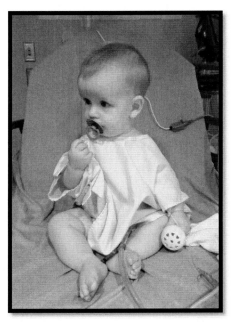

Another Emergency Visit for Another UTI (November 13, 2020)

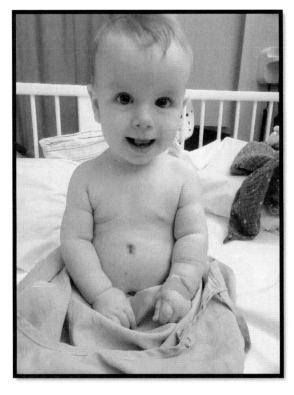

All Smiles After His Biggest Surgery Yet (November 30, 2020)

Prior to the Final Stent Removal (January 15, 2021)

All Surgeries and Procedures Finally Done

JUDE

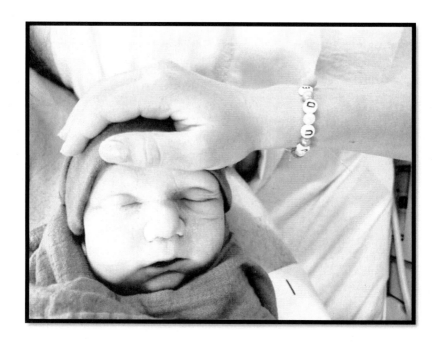

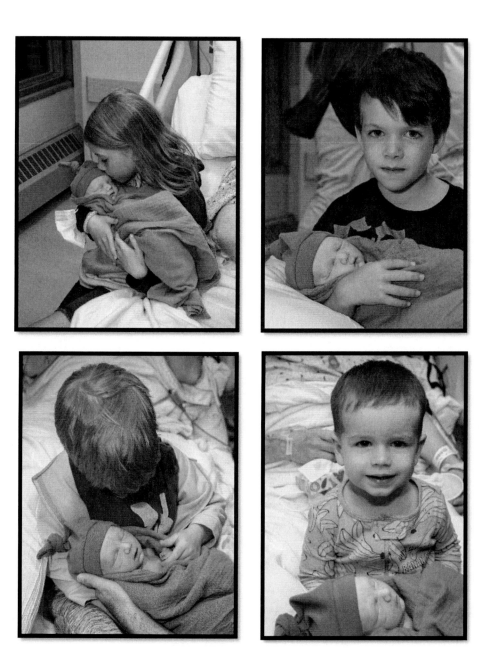

Maggie, Wesley, Dexter & August with Jude

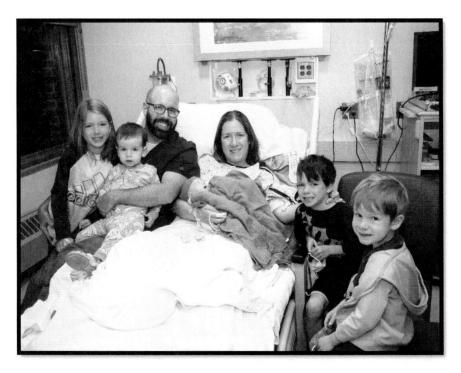

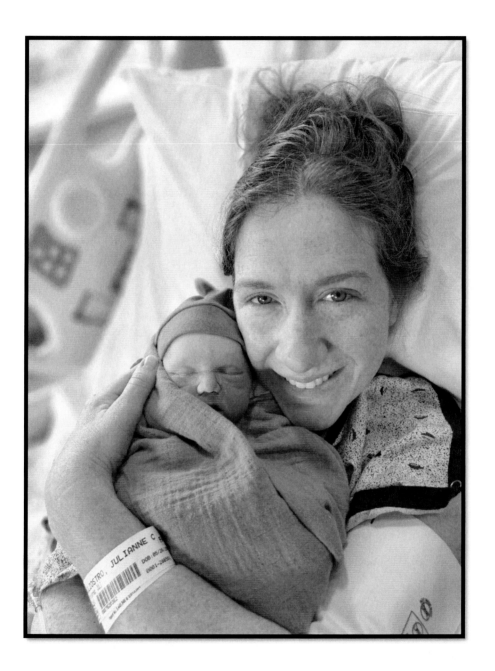

Jude Phineas Cagliostro / July 5, 2022 / 6 lbs / 17 in

...and introducing...

Daphne Rose Cagliostro

November 26, 2023

9 lbs 6 oz / 20.5 in

Made in United States
North Haven, CT
28 July 2024

55552365R00124